Praise for *Effective JavaScript*

"Living up to the expectation of an Effective Software Development Series programming book, *Effective JavaScript* by Dave Herman is a must-read for anyone who wants to do serious JavaScript programming. The book provides detailed explanations of the inner workings of JavaScript, which helps readers take better advantage of the language."

—*Erik Arvidsson, senior software engineer*

"It's uncommon to have a programming language wonk who can speak in such comfortable and friendly language as David does. His walk through the syntax and semantics of JavaScript is both charming and hugely insightful; reminders of gotchas complement realistic use cases, paced at a comfortable curve. You'll find when you finish the book that you've gained a strong and comprehensive sense of mastery."

—*Paul Irish, developer advocate, Google Chrome*

"Before reading *Effective JavaScript*, I thought it would be just another book on how to write better JavaScript. But this book delivers that and so much more—it gives you a deep understanding of the language. And this is crucial. Without that understanding you'll know absolutely nothing whatever about the language itself. You'll only know how other programmers write their code.

"Read this book if you want to become a really good JavaScript developer. I, for one, wish I had it when I first started writing JavaScript."

—*Anton Kovalyov, developer of JSHint*

"If you're looking for a book that gives you formal but highly readable insights into the JavaScript language, look no further. Intermediate JavaScript developers will find a treasure trove of knowledge inside, and even highly skilled JavaScripters are almost guaranteed to learn a thing or ten. For experienced practitioners of other languages looking to dive headfirst into JavaScript, this book is a must-read for quickly getting up to speed. No matter what your background, though, author Dave Herman does a fantastic job of exploring JavaScript—its beautiful parts, its warts, and everything in between."

—*Rebecca Murphey, senior JavaScript developer, Bocoup*

"*Effective JavaScript* is essential reading for anyone who understands that Java-Script is no mere toy and wants to fully grasp the power it has to offer. Dave Herman brings users a deep, studied, and practical understanding of the language, guiding them through example after example to help them come to the same conclusions he has. This is not a book for those looking for shortcuts; rather, it is hard-won experience distilled into a guided tour. It's one of the few books on JavaScript that I'll recommend without hesitation."

—*Alex Russell, TC39 member, software engineer, Google*

"Rarely does anyone have the opportunity   ʼheir
craft. This book is just that—the JavaScript   los-
opher visiting fifth century BC to study witʰ

—*Rick Waldron, JavaScript evangelist, Bocou*

Effective JavaScript

Effective JavaScript

68 SPECIFIC WAYS TO HARNESS THE POWER OF JAVASCRIPT

David Herman

✦✦Addison-Wesley

Upper Saddle River, NJ • Boston • San Francisco • New York • Toronto
Montreal • London • Munich • Paris • Madrid
Capetown • Sydney • Tokyo • Singapore • Mexico City

The publisher offers excellent discounts on this book when ordered in quantity for bulk purchases or special sales, which may include electronic versions and/or custom covers and content particular to your business, training goals, marketing focus, and branding interests. For more information, please contact:

U.S. Corporate and Government Sales
(800) 382-3419
corpsales@pearsontechgroup.com

For sales outside the United States please contact:

International Sales
international@pearsoned.com

Visit us on the Web: informit.com/aw.com

Library of Congress Cataloging-in-Publication Data

Herman, David.
    Effective JavaScript : 68 specific ways to harness the power of JavaScript / David Herman.
        pages   cm
    Includes index.
    ISBN 978-0-321-81218-6 (pbk. : alk. paper) 1. JavaScript (Computer program language)
I. Title.
    QA76.73.J39H47 2012
    005.2'762—dc23

2012035939

ISBN-13:   978-0-321-81218-6
ISBN-10:   0-321-81218-2
Text printed in the United States by RR Donnelley in Crawfordsville, Indiana.
Fourth Printing, April 2015

For Lisa, my love

Contents

Chapter 5: Arrays and Dictionaries   113

Chapter 6: Library and API Design   143

Chapter 7: Concurrency   171

Index   201

Foreword

As is well known at this point, I created JavaScript in ten days in May 1995, under duress and conflicting management imperatives—"make it look like Java," "make it easy for beginners," "make it control almost everything in the Netscape browser."

Apart from getting two big things right (first-class functions, object prototypes), my solution to the challenging requirements and crazy-short schedule was to make JavaScript extremely malleable from the start. I knew developers would have to "patch" the first few versions to fix bugs, and pioneer better approaches than what I had cobbled together in the way of built-in libraries. Where many languages restrict mutability so that, for example, built-in objects cannot be revised or extended at runtime, or standard library name bindings cannot be overridden by assignment, JavaScript allows almost complete alteration of every object.

I believe that this was a good design decision on balance. It clearly presents challenges in certain domains (e.g., safely mixing trusted and untrusted code within the browser's security boundaries). But it was critical to support so-called monkey-patching, whereby developers edited standard objects, both to work around bugs and to retrofit emulations of future functionality into old browsers (the so-called polyfill library shim, which in American English would be called "spackle").

Beyond these sometimes mundane uses, JavaScript's malleability encouraged user innovation networks to form and grow along several more creative paths. Lead users created toolkit or framework libraries patterned on other languages: Prototype on Ruby, MochiKit on Python, Dojo on Java, TIBET on Smalltalk. And then the jQuery library ("New Wave JavaScript"), which seemed to me to be a relative late-comer when I first saw it in 2007, took the JavaScript world by storm by eschewing precedent in other languages while learning from older JavaScript libraries, instead hewing to the "query and do" model of the browser and simplifying it radically.

Lead users and their innovation networks thus developed a JavaScript "home style," which is still being emulated and simplified in other libraries, and also folded into the modern web standardization efforts.

In the course of this evolution, JavaScript has remained backward ("bugward") compatible and of course mutable by default, even with the addition of certain methods in the latest version of the ECMAScript standard for freezing objects against extension and sealing object properties against being overwritten. And JavaScript's evolutionary journey is far from over. Just as with living languages and biological systems, change is a constant over the long term. I still cannot foresee a single "standard library" or coding style sweeping all others before it.

No language is free of quirks or is so restrictive as to dictate universal best practices, and JavaScript is far from quirk-free or restrictionist (more nearly the opposite!). Therefore to be effective, more so than is the case with most other programming languages, JavaScript developers must study and pursue good style, proper usage, and best practices. When considering what is most effective, I believe it's crucial to avoid overreacting and building rigid or dogmatic style guides.

This book takes a balanced approach based on concrete evidence and experience, without swerving into rigidity or excessive prescription. I think it will be a critical aid and trusty guide for many people who seek to write effective JavaScript without sacrificing expressiveness and the freedom to pursue new ideas and paradigms. It's also a focused, fun read with terrific examples.

Finally, I have been privileged to know David Herman since 2006, when I first made contact on behalf of Mozilla to engage him on the Ecma standards body as an invited expert. Dave's deep yet unpretentious expertise and his enthusiasm for JavaScript shine through every page. Bravo!

—*Brendan Eich*

Preface

Learning a programming language requires getting acquainted with its *syntax*, the set of forms and structures that make up legal programs, and *semantics*, the meaning or behavior of those forms. But beyond that, mastering a language requires understanding its *pragmatics*, the ways in which the language's features are used to build effective programs. This latter category can be especially subtle, particularly in a language as flexible and expressive as JavaScript.

This book is concerned with the pragmatics of JavaScript. It is not an introductory book; I assume you have some familiarity with JavaScript in particular and programming in general. There are many excellent introductory books on JavaScript, such as Douglas Crockford's *JavaScript: The Good Parts* and Marijn Haverbeke's *Eloquent JavaScript*. My goal with this book is to help you deepen your understanding of how to use JavaScript effectively to build more predictable, reliable, and maintainable JavaScript applications and libraries.

JavaScript versus ECMAScript

It's helpful to clarify some terminology before diving into the material of this book. This book is about a language almost universally known as JavaScript. Yet the official standard that defines the specification describes a language it calls ECMAScript. The history is convoluted, but it boils down to a matter of trademark: For legal reasons, the standards organization, Ecma International, was unable to use the name "JavaScript" for its standard. (Adding insult to injury, the standards organization changed its name from the original ECMA—an abbreviation for European Computer Manufacturers Association—to Ecma International, without capitalization. By the time of the change, the capitalized name ECMAScript was set in stone.)

Formally, when people refer to ECMAScript they are usually referring to the "ideal" language specified by the Ecma standard. Meanwhile, the name JavaScript could mean anything from the language as it exists in actual practice, to one vendor's specific JavaScript engine. In common usage, people often use the two terms interchangeably. For the sake of clarity and consistency, in this book I will only use *ECMAScript* to talk about the official standard; otherwise, I will refer to the language as *JavaScript*. I also use the common abbreviation *ES5* to refer to the fifth edition of the ECMAScript standard.

On the Web

It's hard to talk about JavaScript without talking about the web. To date, JavaScript is the only programming language with built-in support in all major web browsers for client-side application scripting. Moreover, in recent years, JavaScript has become a popular language for implementing server-side applications with the advent of the Node.js platform.

Nevertheless, this is a book about JavaScript, not about web programming. At times, it's helpful to talk about web-related examples and applications of concepts. But the focus of this book is on the language—its syntax, semantics, and pragmatics—rather than on the APIs and technologies of the web platform.

A Note on Concurrency

A curious aspect of JavaScript is that its behavior in concurrent settings is completely unspecified. Up to and including the fifth edition, the ECMAScript standard says nothing about the behavior of JavaScript programs in an interactive or concurrent environment. Chapter 7 deals with concurrency and so technically describes unofficial features of JavaScript. But in practice, all major JavaScript engines share a common model of concurrency. And working with concurrent and interactive programs is a central unifying concept of JavaScript programming, despite its absence from the standard. In fact, future editions of the ECMAScript standard may officially formalize these shared aspects of the JavaScript concurrency model.

Acknowledgments

This book owes a great deal to JavaScript's inventor, Brendan Eich. I'm deeply grateful to Brendan for inviting me to participate in the standardization of JavaScript and for his mentorship and support in my career at Mozilla.

Much of the material in this book is inspired and informed by excellent blog posts and online articles. I have learned a lot from posts by Ben "cowboy" Alman, Erik Arvidsson, Mathias Bynens, Tim "creationix" Caswell, Michaeljohn "inimino" Clement, Angus Croll, Andrew Dupont, Ariya Hidayat, Steven Levithan, Pan Thomakos, Jeff Walden, and Juriy "kangax" Zaytsev. Of course, the ultimate resource for this book is the ECMAScript specification, which has been tirelessly edited and updated since Edition 5 by Allen Wirfs-Brock. And the Mozilla Developer Network continues to be one of the most impressive and high-quality online resources for JavaScript APIs and features.

I've had many advisors during the course of planning and writing this book. John Resig gave me useful advice on authorship before I began. Blake Kaplan and Patrick Walton helped me collect my thoughts and plan out the organization of the book in the early stages. During the course of the writing, I've gotten great advice from Brian Anderson, Norbert Lindenberg, Sam Tobin-Hochstadt, Rick Waldron, and Patrick Walton.

The staff at Pearson has been a pleasure to work with. Olivia Basegio, Audrey Doyle, Trina MacDonald, Scott Meyers, and Chris Zahn have been attentive to my questions, patient with my delays, and accommodating of my requests. I couldn't imagine a more pleasant first experience with authorship. And I am absolutely honored to contribute to this wonderful series. I've been a fan of *Effective C++* since long before I ever suspected I might have the privilege of writing an Effective book myself.

I couldn't believe my good fortune at finding such a dream team of technical editors. I'm honored that Erik Arvidsson, Rebecca Murphey, Rick Waldron, and Richard Worth agreed to edit this book, and they've provided me with invaluable critiques and suggestions. On more than one occasion they saved me from some truly embarrassing errors.

Writing a book was more intimidating than I expected. I might have lost my nerve if it weren't for the support of friends and colleagues. I don't know if they knew it at the time, but Andy Denmark, Rick Waldron, and Travis Winfrey gave me the encouragement I needed in moments of doubt.

The vast majority of this book was written at the fabulous Java Beach Café in San Francisco's beautiful Parkside neighborhood. The staff members all know my name and know what I'm going to order before I order it. I am grateful to them for providing a cozy place to work and keeping me fed and caffeinated.

My fuzzy little feline friend Schmoopy tried his best to contribute to this book. At least, he kept hopping onto my lap and sitting in front of the screen. (This *might* have something to do with the warmth of the laptop.) Schmoopy has been my loyal buddy since 2006, and I can't imagine my life without the little furball.

My entire family has been supportive and excited about this project from beginning to end. Sadly, my grandparents Frank and Miriam Slamar both passed away before I could share the final product with them. But they were excited and proud for me, and there's a little piece of my boyhood experiences writing BASIC programs with Frank in this book.

Finally, I owe the love of my life, Lisa Silveria, more than could ever be repaid in an introduction.

About the Author

David Herman is a senior researcher at Mozilla Research. He holds a BA in computer science from Grinnell College and an MS and PhD in computer science from Northeastern University. David serves on Ecma TC39, the committee responsible for the standardization of JavaScript.

Accustoming Yourself to JavaScript

JavaScript was designed to feel familiar. With syntax reminiscent of Java and constructs common to many scripting languages (such as functions, arrays, dictionaries, and regular expressions), JavaScript seems like a quick learn to anyone with a little programming experience. And for novice programmers, it's possible to get started writing programs with relatively little training thanks to the small number of core concepts in the language.

As approachable as JavaScript is, mastering the language takes more time, and requires a deeper understanding of its semantics, its idiosyncrasies, and its most effective idioms. Each chapter of this book covers a different thematic area of effective JavaScript. This first chapter begins with some of the most fundamental topics.

Item 1: Know Which JavaScript You Are Using

Like most successful technologies, JavaScript has evolved over time. Originally marketed as a complement to Java for programming interactive web pages, JavaScript eventually supplanted Java as the web's dominant programming language. JavaScript's popularity led to its formalization in 1997 as an international standard, known officially as ECMAScript. Today there are many competing implementations of JavaScript providing conformance to various versions of the ECMA-Script standard.

The third edition of the ECMAScript standard (commonly referred to as ES3), which was finalized in 1999, continues to be the most widely adopted version of JavaScript. The next major advancement to the standard was Edition 5, or ES5, which was released in 2009. ES5 introduced a number of new features as well as standardizing some widely supported but previously unspecified features. Because ES5 support is not yet ubiquitous, I will point out throughout this book whenever a particular Item or piece of advice is specific to ES5.

In addition to multiple editions of the standard, there are a number of nonstandard features that are supported by some JavaScript implementations but not others. For example, many JavaScript engines support a `const` keyword for defining variables, yet the ECMAScript standard does not provide any definition for the syntax or behavior of `const`. Moreover, the behavior of `const` differs from implementation to implementation. In some cases, `const` variables are prevented from being updated:

```
const PI = 3.141592653589793;
PI = "modified!";
PI; // 3.141592653589793
```

Other implementations simply treat `const` as a synonym for `var`:

```
const PI = 3.141592653589793;
PI = "modified!";
PI; // "modified!"
```

Given JavaScript's long history and diversity of implementations, it can be difficult to keep track of which features are available on which platform. Compounding this problem is the fact that JavaScript's primary ecosystem—the web browser—does not give programmers control over which version of JavaScript is available to execute their code. Since end users may use different versions of different web browsers, web programs have to be written carefully to work consistently across all browsers.

On the other hand, JavaScript is not exclusively used for client-side web programming. Other uses include server-side programs, browser extensions, and scripting for mobile and desktop applications. In some of these cases, you may have a much more specific version of JavaScript available to you. For these cases, it makes sense to take advantage of additional features specific to the platform's particular implementation of JavaScript.

This book is concerned primarily with standard features of JavaScript. But it is also important to discuss certain widely supported but nonstandard features. When dealing with newer standards or nonstandard features, it is critical to understand whether your applications will run in environments that support those features. Otherwise, you may find yourself in situations where your applications work as intended on your own computer or testing infrastructure, but fail when you deploy them to users running your application in different environments. For example, `const` may work fine when tested on an engine that supports the nonstandard feature but then fail with a syntax error when deployed in a web browser that does not recognize the keyword.

ES5 introduced another versioning consideration with its *strict mode.* This feature allows you to opt in to a restricted version of JavaScript that disallows some of the more problematic or error-prone features of the full language. The syntax was designed to be backward-compatible so that environments that do not implement the strict-mode checks can still execute strict code. Strict mode is enabled in a program by adding a special string constant at the very beginning of the program:

```
"use strict";
```

Similarly, you can enable strict mode in a function by placing the directive at the beginning of the function body:

```
function f(x) {
    "use strict";
    // ...
}
```

The use of a string literal for the directive syntax looks a little strange, but it has the benefit of backward compatibility: Evaluating a string literal has no side effects, so an ES3 engine executes the directive as an innocuous statement—it evaluates the string and then discards its value immediately. This makes it possible to write code in strict mode that runs in older JavaScript engines, but with a crucial limitation: The old engines will not perform any of the checks of strict mode. If you don't test in an ES5 environment, it's all too easy to write code that will be rejected when run in an ES5 environment:

```
function f(x) {
    "use strict";
    var arguments = []; // error: redefinition of arguments
    // ...
}
```

Redefining the `arguments` variable is disallowed in strict mode, but an environment that does not implement the strict-mode checks will accept this code. Deploying this code in production would then cause the program to fail in environments that implement ES5. For this reason you should always test strict code in fully compliant ES5 environments.

One pitfall of using strict mode is that the `"use strict"` directive is only recognized at the top of a script or function, which makes it sensitive to *script concatenation,* where large applications are developed in separate files that are then combined into a single file for deploying in production. Consider one file that expects to be in strict mode:

```
// file1.js
"use strict";
function f() {
    // ...
}
// ...
```

and another file that expects not to be in strict mode:

```
// file2.js
// no strict-mode directive
function g() {
    var arguments = [];
    // ...
}
// ...
```

How can we concatenate these two files correctly? If we start with file1.js, then the whole combined file is in strict mode:

```
// file1.js
"use strict";
function f() {
    // ...
}
// ...
// file2.js
// no strict-mode directive
function f() {
    var arguments = []; // error: redefinition of arguments
    // ...
}
// ...
```

And if we start with file2.js, then none of the combined file is in strict mode:

```
// file2.js
// no strict-mode directive
function g() {
    var arguments = [];
    // ...
}
// ...
// file1.js
```

```
"use strict";
function f() { // no longer strict
    // ...
}
// ...
```

In your own projects, you could stick to a "strict-mode only" or "non-strict-mode only" policy, but if you want to write robust code that can be combined with a wide variety of code, you have a few alternatives.

Never concatenate strict files and nonstrict files. This is probably the easiest solution, but it of course restricts the amount of control you have over the file structure of your application or library. At best, you have to deploy two separate files, one containing all the strict files and one containing the nonstrict files.

Concatenate files by wrapping their bodies in immediately invoked function expressions. Item 13 provides an in-depth explanation of immediately invoked function expressions (IIFEs), but in short, by wrapping each file's contents in a function, they can be independently interpreted in different modes. The concatenated version of the above example would look like this:

```
// no strict-mode directive
(function() {
    // file1.js
    "use strict";
    function f() {
        // ...
    }
    // ...
})();
(function() {
    // file2.js
    // no strict-mode directive
    function f() {
        var arguments = [];
        // ...
    }
    // ...
})();
```

Since each file's contents are placed in a separate scope, the strict-mode directive (or lack of one) only affects that file's contents. For this approach to work, however, the contents of files cannot assume that they are interpreted at global scope. For example, var and function declarations do not persist as global variables (see Item 8 for more on globals). This happens to be the case with popular *module systems,* which manage files and dependencies by automatically placing each module's contents in a separate function. Since files are all placed in local scopes, each file can make its own decision about whether to use strict mode.

Write your files so that they behave the same in either mode. To write a library that works in as many contexts as possible, you cannot assume that it will be placed inside the contents of a function by a script concatenation tool, nor can you assume whether the client codebase will be strict or nonstrict. The simplest way to structure your code for maximum compatibility is to write for strict mode but explicitly wrap the contents of all your code in functions that enable strict mode locally. This is similar to the previous solution, in that you wrap each file's contents in an IIFE, but in this case you write the IIFE by hand instead of trusting the concatenation tool or module system to do it for you, and explicitly opt in to strict mode:

```
(function() {
    "use strict";
    function f() {
        // ...
    }
    // ...
})();
```

Notice that this code is treated as strict regardless of whether it is concatenated in a strict or nonstrict context. By contrast, a function that does not opt in to strict mode will still be treated as strict if it is concatenated after strict code. So the more universally compatible option is to write in strict mode.

Things to Remember

✦ Decide which versions of JavaScript your application supports.

✦ Be sure that any JavaScript features you use are supported by all environments where your application runs.

✦ Always test strict code in environments that perform the strict-mode checks.

✦ Beware of concatenating scripts that differ in their expectations about strict mode.

Item 2: Understand JavaScript's Floating-Point Numbers

Most programming languages have several types of numeric data, but JavaScript gets away with just one. You can see this reflected in the behavior of the `typeof` operator, which classifies integers and floating-point numbers alike simply as numbers:

```
typeof 17;   // "number"
typeof 98.6; // "number"
typeof -2.1; // "number"
```

In fact, all numbers in JavaScript are *double-precision floating-point* numbers, that is, the 64-bit encoding of numbers specified by the IEEE 754 standard—commonly known as "doubles." If this fact leaves you wondering what happened to the integers, keep in mind that doubles can represent integers perfectly with up to 53 bits of precision. All of the integers from $-9,007,199,254,740,992$ (-2^{53}) to $9,007,199,254,740,992$ (2^{53}) are valid doubles. So it's perfectly possible to do integer arithmetic in JavaScript, despite the lack of a distinct integer type.

Most arithmetic operators work with integers, real numbers, or a combination of the two:

```
0.1 * 1.9  // 0.19
-99 + 100; // 1
21 - 12.3; // 8.7
2.5 / 5;   // 0.5
21 % 8;    // 5
```

The bitwise arithmetic operators, however, are special. Rather than operating on their arguments directly as floating-point numbers, they implicitly convert them to 32-bit integers. (To be precise, they are treated as 32-bit, *big-endian, two's complement* integers.) For example, take the bitwise OR expression:

```
8 | 1; // 9
```

This simple-looking expression actually requires several steps to evaluate. As always, the JavaScript numbers 8 and 1 are doubles. But they can also be represented as 32-bit integers, that is, sequences of thirty-two 1's and 0's. As a 32-bit integer, the number 8 looks like this:

```
00000000000000000000000000001000
```

You can see this for yourself by using the `toString` method of numbers:

```
(8).toString(2); // "1000"
```

The argument to `toString` specifies the *radix*, in this case indicating a base 2 (i.e., binary) representation. The result drops the extra 0 bits on the left since they don't affect the value.

The integer 1 is represented in 32 bits as:

00000000000000000000000000000001

The bitwise OR expression combines the two bit sequences by keeping any 1 bits found in either input, resulting in the bit pattern:

00000000000000000000000000001001

This sequence represents the integer 9. You can verify this by using the standard library function `parseInt`, again with a radix of 2:

```
parseInt("1001", 2); // 9
```

(The leading 0 bits are unnecessary since, again, they don't affect the result.)

All of the bitwise operators work the same way, converting their inputs to integers and performing their operations on the integer bit patterns before converting the results back to standard JavaScript floating-point numbers. In general, these conversions require extra work in JavaScript engines: Since numbers are stored as floating-point, they have to be converted to integers and then back to floating-point again. However, optimizing compilers can sometimes infer when arithmetic expressions and even variables work exclusively with integers, and avoid the extra conversions by storing the data internally as integers.

A final note of caution about floating-point numbers: If they don't make you at least a little nervous, they probably should. Floating-point numbers look deceptively familiar, but they are notoriously inaccurate. Even some of the simplest-looking arithmetic can produce inaccurate results:

```
0.1 + 0.2; // 0.30000000000000004
```

While 64 bits of precision is reasonably large, doubles can still only represent a finite set of numbers, rather than the infinite set of real numbers. Floating-point arithmetic can only produce approximate results, rounding to the nearest representable real number. When you perform a sequence of calculations, these rounding errors can accumulate, leading to less and less accurate results. Rounding also causes surprising deviations from the kind of properties we usually expect of arithmetic. For example, real numbers are *associative,* meaning that for any real numbers x, y, and z, it's always the case that $(x + y) + z = x + (y + z)$.

But this is not always true of floating-point numbers:

```
(0.1 + 0.2) + 0.3; // 0.6000000000000001
0.1 + (0.2 + 0.3); // 0.6
```

Floating-point numbers offer a trade-off between accuracy and performance. When accuracy matters, it's critical to be aware of their limitations. One useful workaround is to work with integer values wherever possible, since they can be represented without rounding. When doing calculations with money, programmers often scale numbers up to work with the currency's smallest denomination so that they can compute with whole numbers. For example, if the above calculation were measured in dollars, we could work with whole numbers of cents instead:

```
(10 + 20) + 30; // 60
10 + (20 + 30); // 60
```

With integers, you still have to take care that all calculations fit within the range between -2^{53} and 2^{53}, but you don't have to worry about rounding errors.

Things to Remember

✦ JavaScript numbers are double-precision floating-point numbers.

✦ Integers in JavaScript are just a subset of doubles rather than a separate datatype.

✦ Bitwise operators treat numbers as if they were 32-bit signed integers.

✦ Be aware of limitations of precisions in floating-point arithmetic.

Item 3: Beware of Implicit Coercions

JavaScript can be surprisingly forgiving when it comes to type errors. Many languages consider an expression like

```
3 + true; // 4
```

to be an error, because boolean expressions such as true are incompatible with arithmetic. In a statically typed language, a program with such an expression would not even be allowed to run. In some dynamically typed languages, while the program would run, such an expression would throw an exception. JavaScript not only allows the program to run, but it happily produces the result 4!

There are a handful of cases in JavaScript where providing the wrong type produces an immediate error, such as calling a nonfunction or attempting to select a property of null:

```
"hello"(1); // error: not a function
null.x;     // error: cannot read property 'x' of null
```

But in many other cases, rather than raising an error, JavaScript *coerces* a value to the expected type by following various automatic conversion protocols. For example, the arithmetic operators -, *, /, and % all attempt to convert their arguments to numbers before doing their calculation. The operator + is subtler, because it is overloaded to perform either numeric addition or string concatenation, depending on the types of its arguments:

```
2 + 3;                 // 5
"hello" + " world"; // "hello world"
```

Now, what happens when you combine a number and a string? Java-Script breaks the tie in favor of strings, converting the number to a string:

```
"2" + 3; // "23"
2 + "3"; // "23"
```

Mixing types like this can sometimes be confusing, especially because it's sensitive to the order of operations. Take the expression:

```
1 + 2 + "3";     // "33"
```

Since addition groups to the left (i.e., is *left-associative*), this is the same as:

```
(1 + 2) + "3";   // "33"
```

By contrast, the expression

```
1 + "2" + 3;     // "123"
```

evaluates to the string "123"—again, left-associativity dictates that the expression is equivalent to wrapping the left-hand addition in parentheses:

```
(1 + "2") + 3;   // "123"
```

The bitwise operations not only convert to numbers but to the subset of numbers that can be represented as 32-bit integers, as discussed in Item 2. These include the bitwise arithmetic operators (~, &, ^, and |) and the shift operators (<<, >>, and >>>).

These coercions can be seductively convenient—for example, for automatically converting strings that come from user input, a text file, or a network stream:

```
"17" * 3;  // 51
"8" | "1"; // 9
```

But coercions can also hide errors. A variable that turns out to be null will not fail in an arithmetic calculation, but silently convert to 0; an undefined variable will convert to the special floating-point value NaN (the paradoxically named "not a number" number—blame the IEEE floating-point standard!). Rather than immediately throwing an exception, these coercions cause the calculation to continue with often confusing and unpredictable results. Frustratingly, it's particularly difficult even to test for the NaN value, for two reasons. First, JavaScript follows the IEEE floating-point standard's head-scratching requirement that NaN be treated as unequal to itself. So testing whether a value is equal to NaN doesn't work at all:

```
var x = NaN;
x === NaN;    // false
```

Moreover, the standard isNaN library function is not very reliable because it comes with its own implicit coercion, converting its argument to a number before testing the value. (A more accurate name for isNaN probably would have been coercesToNaN.) If you already know that a value is a number, you can test it for NaN with isNaN:

```
isNaN(NaN); // true
```

But other values that are definitely not NaN, yet are nevertheless coercible to NaN, are indistinguishable to isNaN:

```
isNaN("foo");             // true
isNaN(undefined);         // true
isNaN({});                // true
isNaN({ valueOf: "foo" }); // true
```

Luckily there's an idiom that is both reliable and concise—if somewhat unintuitive—for testing for NaN. Since NaN is the only JavaScript value that is treated as unequal to itself, you can always test if a value is NaN by checking it for equality to itself:

```
var a = NaN;
a !== a;                  // true
var b = "foo";
b !== b;                  // false
```

```
var c = undefined;
c !== c;                    // false
var d = {};
d !== d;                    // false
var e = { valueOf: "foo" };
e !== e;                    // false
```

You can also abstract this pattern into a clearly named utility function:

```
function isReallyNaN(x) {
    return x !== x;
}
```

But testing a value for inequality to itself is so concise that it's commonly used without a helper function, so it's important to recognize and understand.

Silent coercions can make debugging a broken program particularly frustrating, since they cover up errors and make them harder to diagnose. When a calculation goes wrong, the best approach to debugging is to inspect the intermediate results of a calculation, working back to the last point before things went wrong. From there, you can inspect the arguments of each operation, looking for arguments of the wrong type. Depending on the bug, it could be a logical error, such as using the wrong arithmetic operator, or a type error, such as passing the undefined value instead of a number.

Objects can also be coerced to primitives. This is most commonly used for converting to strings:

```
"the Math object: " + Math; // "the Math object: [object Math]"
"the JSON object: " + JSON; // "the JSON object: [object JSON]"
```

Objects are converted to strings by implicitly calling their toString method. You can test this out by calling it yourself:

```
Math.toString(); // "[object Math]"
JSON.toString(); // "[object JSON]"
```

Similarly, objects can be converted to numbers via their valueOf method. You can control the type conversion of objects by defining these methods:

```
"J" + { toString: function() { return "S"; } }; // "JS"
2 * { valueOf: function() { return 3; } };       // 6
```

Once again, things get tricky when you consider that + is overloaded to perform both string concatenation and addition. Specifically, when an object contains both a toString and a valueOf method, it's not obvious which method + should call: It's supposed to choose between concatenation and addition based on types, but with implicit coercion, the types are not actually given! JavaScript resolves this ambiguity by blindly choosing valueOf over toString. But this means that if someone intends to perform a string concatenation with an object, it can behave unexpectedly:

```js
var obj = {
    toString: function() {
        return "[object MyObject]";
    },
    valueOf: function() {
        return 17;
    }
};
"object: " + obj; // "object: 17"
```

The moral of this story is that valueOf was really only designed to be used for objects that represent numeric values such as Number objects. For these objects, the toString and valueOf methods return consistent results—a string representation or numeric representation of the same number—so the overloaded + always behaves consistently regardless of whether the object is used for concatenation or addition. In general, coercion to strings is far more common and useful than coercion to numbers. It's best to avoid valueOf unless your object really is a numeric abstraction and obj.toString() produces a string representation of obj.valueOf().

The last kind of coercion is sometimes known as *truthiness*. Operators such as if, ||, and && logically work with boolean values, but actually accept any values. JavaScript values are interpreted as boolean values according to a simple implicit coercion. Most JavaScript values are *truthy*, that is, implicitly coerced to true. This includes all objects—unlike string and number coercion, truthiness does not involve implicitly invoking any coercion methods. There are exactly seven *falsy* values: false, 0, -0, "", NaN, null, and undefined. All other values are truthy. Since numbers and strings can be falsy, it's not always safe to use truthiness to check whether a function argument or object property is defined. Consider a function that takes optional arguments with default values:

```js
function point(x, y) {
    if (!x) {
        x = 320;
    }
```

```
  if (!y) {
      y = 240;
  }
  return { x: x, y: y };
}
```

This function ignores any falsy arguments, which includes 0:

```
point(0, 0); // { x: 320, y: 240 }
```

The more precise way to check for undefined is to use typeof:

```
function point(x, y) {
    if (typeof x === "undefined") {
        x = 320;
    }
    if (typeof y === "undefined") {
        y = 240;
    }
    return { x: x, y: y };
}
```

This version of point correctly distinguishes between 0 and undefined:

```
point();     // { x: 320, y: 240 }
point(0, 0); // { x: 0, y: 0 }
```

Another approach is to compare to undefined:

```
if (x === undefined) { ... }
```

Item 54 discusses the implications of truthiness testing for library and API design.

Things to Remember

+ Type errors can be silently hidden by implicit coercions.

+ The + operator is overloaded to do addition or string concatenation depending on its argument types.

+ Objects are coerced to numbers via valueOf and to strings via toString.

+ Objects with valueOf methods should implement a toString method that provides a string representation of the number produced by valueOf.

+ Use typeof or comparison to undefined rather than truthiness to test for undefined values.

Item 4: Prefer Primitives to Object Wrappers

In addition to objects, JavaScript has five types of primitive values: booleans, numbers, strings, null, and undefined. (Confusingly, the typeof operator reports the type of null as "object", but the ECMA-Script standard describes it as a distinct type.) At the same time, the standard library provides constructors for wrapping booleans, numbers, and strings as objects. You can create a String object that wraps a string value:

```
var s = new String("hello");
```

In some ways, a String object behaves similarly to the string value it wraps. You can concatenate it with other values to create strings:

```
s + " world"; // "hello world"
```

You can extract its indexed substrings:

```
s[4]; // "o"
```

But unlike primitive strings, a String object is a true object:

```
typeof "hello"; // "string"
typeof s;       // "object"
```

This is an important difference, because it means that you can't compare the contents of two distinct String objects using built-in operators:

```
var s1 = new String("hello");
var s2 = new String("hello");
s1 === s2; // false
```

Since each String object is a separate object, it is only ever equal to itself. The same is true for the nonstrict equality operator:

```
s1 == s2; // false
```

Since these wrappers don't behave quite right, they don't serve much of a purpose. The main justification for their existence is their utility methods. JavaScript makes these convenient to use with another implicit coercion: You can extract properties and call methods of a primitive value, and it acts as though you had wrapped the value with its corresponding object type. For example, the String prototype object has a toUpperCase method, which converts a string to uppercase. You can use this method on a primitive string value:

```
"hello".toUpperCase(); // "HELLO"
```

A strange consequence of this implicit wrapping is that you can set properties on primitive values with essentially no effect:

```
"hello".someProperty = 17;
"hello".someProperty; // undefined
```

Since the implicit wrapping produces a new String object each time it occurs, the update to the first wrapper object has no lasting effect. There's really no point to setting properties on primitive values, but it's worth being aware of this behavior. It turns out to be another instance of where JavaScript can hide type errors: If you set properties on what you expect to be an object, but use a primitive value by mistake, your program will simply silently ignore the update and continue. This can easily cause the error to go undetected and make it harder to diagnose.

Things to Remember

✦ Object wrappers for primitive types do not have the same behavior as their primitive values when compared for equality.

✦ Getting and setting properties on primitives implicitly creates object wrappers.

Item 5: Avoid using == with Mixed Types

What would you expect to be the value of this expression?

```
"1.0e0" == { valueOf: function() { return true; } };
```

These two seemingly unrelated values are actually considered equivalent by the == operator because, like the implicit coercions described in Item 3, they are both converted to numbers before being compared. The string "1.0e0" parses as the number 1, and the object is converted to a number by calling its valueOf method and converting the result (true) to a number, which also produces 1.

It's tempting to use these coercions for tasks like reading a field from a web form and comparing it with a number:

```
var today = new Date();

if (form.month.value == (today.getMonth() + 1) &&
    form.day.value == today.getDate()) {
    // happy birthday!
    // ...
}
```

But it's actually easy to convert values to numbers *explicitly* using the Number function or the unary + operator:

```
var today = new Date();

if (+form.month.value == (today.getMonth() + 1) &&
    +form.day.value == today.getDate()) {
    // happy birthday!
    // ...
}
```

This is clearer, because it conveys to readers of your code exactly what conversion is being applied, without requiring them to memorize the conversion rules. An even better alternative is to use the *strict equality* operator:

```
var today = new Date();

if (+form.month.value === (today.getMonth() + 1) && // strict
    +form.day.value === today.getDate()) {          // strict
    // happy birthday!
    // ...
}
```

When the two arguments are of the same type, there's no difference in behavior between == and ===. So if you know that the arguments are of the same type, they are interchangeable. But using strict equality is a good way to make it clear to readers that there is no conversion involved in the comparison. Otherwise, you require readers to recall the exact coercion rules to decipher your code's behavior.

As it turns out, these coercion rules are not at all obvious. Table 1.1 contains the coercion rules for the == operator when its arguments are of different types. The rules are symmetric: For example, the first rule applies to both null == undefined and undefined == null. Most of the time, the conversions attempt to produce numbers. But the rules get subtle when they deal with objects. The operation tries to convert an object to a primitive value by calling its valueOf and toString methods, using the first primitive value it gets. Even more subtly, Date objects try these two methods in the opposite order.

The == operator deceptively appears to paper over different representations of data. This kind of error correction is sometimes known as *"do what I mean" semantics.* But computers cannot really read your mind. There are too many data representations in the world for JavaScript

Table 1.1 Coercion Rules for the == Operator

Argument Type 1	Argument Type 2	Coercions
null	undefined	None; always true
null or undefined	Any other than null or undefined	None; always false
Primitive string, number, or boolean	Date object	Primitive => number, Date object => primitive (try toString and then valueOf)
Primitive string, number, or boolean	Non-Date object	Primitive => number, non-Date object => primitive (try valueOf and then toString)
Primitive string, number, or boolean	Primitive string, number, or boolean	Primitive => number

to know which one you are using. For example, you might hope that you could compare a string containing a date to a Date object:

```
var date = new Date("1999/12/31");
date == "1999/12/31"; // false
```

This particular example fails because converting a Date object to a string produces a different format than the one used in the example:

```
date.toString(); // "Fri Dec 31 1999 00:00:00 GMT-0800 (PST)"
```

But the mistake is symptomatic of a more general misunderstanding of coercions. The == operator does not infer and unify arbitrary data formats. It requires both you and your readers to understand its subtle coercion rules. A better policy is to make the conversions explicit with custom application logic and use the strict equality operator:

```
function toYMD(date) {
    var y = date.getYear() + 1900, // year is 1900-indexed
        m = date.getMonth() + 1,   // month is 0-indexed
        d = date.getDate();
    return y
        + "/" + (m < 10 ? "0" + m : m)
        + "/" + (d < 10 ? "0" + d : d);
}
toYMD(date) === "1999/12/31"; // true
```

Making conversions explicit ensures that you don't mix up the coercion rules of ==, and—even better—relieves your readers from having to look up the coercion rules or memorize them.

Things to Remember

+ The == operator applies a confusing set of implicit coercions when its arguments are of different types.

+ Use === to make it clear to your readers that your comparison does not involve any implicit coercions.

+ Use your own explicit coercions when comparing values of different types to make your program's behavior clearer.

Item 6: Learn the Limits of Semicolon Insertion

One of JavaScript's conveniences is the ability to leave off statement-terminating semicolons. Dropping semicolons results in a pleasantly lightweight aesthetic:

```javascript
function Point(x, y) {
    this.x = x || 0
    this.y = y || 0
}

Point.prototype.isOrigin = function() {
    return this.x === 0 && this.y === 0
}
```

This works thanks to *automatic semicolon insertion*, a program parsing technique that infers omitted semicolons in certain contexts, effectively "inserting" the semicolon into the program for you automatically. The ECMAScript standard precisely specifies the semicolon insertion mechanism, so optional semicolons are portable between JavaScript engines.

But similar to the implicit coercions of Items 3 and 5, semicolon insertion has its pitfalls, and you simply can't avoid learning its rules. Even if you never omit semicolons, there are additional restrictions in the JavaScript syntax that are consequences of semicolon insertion. The good news is that once you learn the rules of semicolon insertion, you may find it liberating to drop unnecessary semicolons.

The first rule of semicolon insertion is:

Semicolons are only ever inserted before a } token, after one or more newlines, or at the end of the program input.

In other words, you can only leave out semicolons at the end of a line, block, or program. So the following are legal functions:

```
function square(x) {
    var n = +x
    return n * n
}
function area(r) { r = +r; return Math.PI * r * r }
function add1(x) { return x + 1 }
```

But this is not:

```
function area(r) { r = +r return Math.PI * r * r } // error
```

The second rule of semicolon insertion is:

Semicolons are only ever inserted when the next input token cannot be parsed.

In other words, semicolon insertion is an *error correction* mechanism. As a simple example, this snippet:

```
a = b
(f());
```

parses just fine as a single statement, equivalent to:

```
a = b(f());
```

That is, no semicolon is inserted. By contrast, this snippet:

```
a = b
f();
```

is parsed as two separate statements, because

```
a = b f();
```

is a parse error.

This rule has an unfortunate implication: You always have to pay attention to the start of the next statement to detect whether you can legally omit a semicolon. You can't leave off a statement's semicolon if the next line's initial token could be interpreted as a continuation of the statement.

There are exactly five problematic characters to watch out for: (, [, +, -, and /. Each one of these can act either as an expression operator or as the prefix of a statement, depending on the context. So watch out for statements that end with an expression, like the assignment statement above. If the next line starts with any of the five problematic characters, no semicolon will be inserted. By far, the most common scenario where this occurs is a statement beginning with a parenthesis, like the example above. Another common scenario is an array literal:

```
a = b
["r", "g", "b"].forEach(function(key) {
    background[key] = foreground[key] / 2;
});
```

This looks like two statements: an assignment followed by a statement that calls a function on the strings "r", "g", and "b" in order. But because the statement begins with [, it parses as a single statement, equivalent to:

```
a = b["r", "g", "b"].forEach(function(key) {
    background[key] = foreground[key] / 2;
});
```

If that bracketed expression looks odd, remember that JavaScript allows comma-separated expressions, which evaluate from left to right and return the value of their last subexpression: in this case, the string "b".

The +, -, and / tokens are less commonly found at the beginning of statements, but it's not unheard of. The case of / is particularly subtle: At the start of a statement, it is actually not an entire token but the beginning of a regular expression token:

```
/Error/i.test(str) && fail();
```

This statement tests a string with the case-insensitive regular expression /Error/i. If a match is found, the statement calls the fail function. But if this code follows an unterminated assignment:

```
a = b
/Error/i.test(str) && fail();
```

then the code parses as a single statement equivalent to:

```
a = b / Error / i.test(str) && fail();
```

In other words, the initial / token parses as the division operator!

Experienced JavaScript programmers learn to look at the line following a statement whenever they want to leave out a semicolon, to make sure the statement won't be parsed incorrectly. They also take care when refactoring. For example, a perfectly correct program with three inferred semicolons:

```
a = b      // semicolon inferred
var x      // semicolon inferred
(f())      // semicolon inferred
```

can unexpectedly change to a different program with only two inferred semicolons:

```
var x      // semicolon inferred
a = b      // no semicolon inferred
(f())      // semicolon inferred
```

Even though it should be equivalent to move the var statement up one line (see Item 12 for details of variable scope), the fact that b is followed by a parenthesis means that the program is mis-parsed as:

```
var x;
a = b(f());
```

The upshot is that you always need to be aware of omitted semicolons and check the beginning of the following line for tokens that disable semicolon insertion. Alternatively, you can follow a rule of always prefixing statements beginning with (, [, +, -, or / with an extra semicolon. For example, the previous example can be changed to protect the parenthesized function call:

```
a = b      // semicolon inferred
var x      // semicolon on next line
;(f())     // semicolon inferred
```

Now it's safe to move the var declaration to the top without fear of changing the program:

```
var x      // semicolon inferred
a = b      // semicolon on next line
;(f())     // semicolon inferred
```

Another common scenario where omitted semicolons can cause problems is with script concatenation (see Item 1). Each file might consist of a large function call expression (see Item 13 for more about immediately invoked function expressions):

```
// file1.js
(function() {
    // ...
})()

// file2.js
(function() {
    // ...
})()
```

When each file is loaded as a separate program, a semicolon is automatically inserted at the end, turning the function call into a statement. But when the files are concatenated:

```
(function() {
    // ...
})()
(function() {
    // ...
})()
```

the result is treated as one single statement, equivalent to:

```
(function() {
    // ...
})()(function() {
    // ...
})();
```

The upshot: Omitting a semicolon from a statement requires being aware of not only the next token in the current file, but any token that *might* follow the statement after script concatenation. Similar to the approach described above, you can protect scripts against careless concatenation by defensively prefixing every file with an extra semicolon, at least if its first statement begins with one of the five vulnerable characters (, [, +, -, or /:

```
// file1.js
;(function() {
    // ...
})()
```

```
// file2.js
;(function() {
    // ...
})()
```

This ensures that even if the preceding file omits its final semicolon, the combined results will still be treated as separate statements:

```
;(function() {
    // ...
})()
;(function() {
    // ...
})()
```

Of course, it's better if the script concatenation process adds extra semicolons between files automatically. But not all concatenation tools are well written, so your safest bet is to add semicolons defensively.

At this point, you might be thinking, "This is too much to worry about. I'll just never omit semicolons and I'll be fine." Not so: There are also cases where JavaScript will forcibly insert a semicolon even though it might appear that there is no parse error. These are the so-called *restricted productions* of the JavaScript syntax, where no newline is allowed to appear between two tokens. The most hazardous case is the `return` statement, which must not contain a newline between the `return` keyword and its optional argument. So the statement:

```
return { };
```

returns a new object, whereas the code snippet:

```
return
{ };
```

parses as three separate statements, equivalent to:

```
return;
{ }
;
```

In other words, the newline following the `return` keyword forces an automatic semicolon insertion, which parses as a `return` with no argument followed by an empty block and an empty statement. The other restricted productions are

- A `throw` statement
- A `break` or `continue` statement with an explicit label
- A postfix ++ or -- operator

The purpose of the last rule is to disambiguate code snippets such as the following:

```
a
++
b
```

Since ++ can serve as either a prefix or a suffix, but the latter cannot be preceded by a newline, this parses as:

```
a; ++b;
```

The third and final rule of semicolon insertion is:

Semicolons are never inserted as separators in the head of a for *loop or as empty statements.*

This simply means that you must always explicitly include the semi-colons in a `for` loop's head. Otherwise, input such as this:

```
for (var i = 0, total = 1 // parse error
     i < n
     i++) {
    total *= i
}
```

results in a parse error. Similarly, a loop with an empty body requires an explicit semicolon. Otherwise, leaving off the semicolon results in a parse error:

```
function infiniteLoop() { while (true) } // parse error
```

So this is one case where the semicolon is required:

```
function infiniteLoop() { while (true); }
```

Things to Remember

✦ Semicolons are only ever inferred before a }, at the end of a line, or at the end of a program.

✦ Semicolons are only ever inferred when the next token cannot be parsed.

✦ Never omit a semicolon before a statement beginning with (, [, +, -, or /.

✦ When concatenating scripts, insert semicolons explicitly between scripts.

✦ Never put a newline before the argument to `return`, `throw`, `break`, `continue`, `++`, or `--`.

✦ Semicolons are never inferred as separators in the head of a `for` loop or as empty statements.

Item 7: Think of Strings As Sequences of 16-Bit Code Units

Unicode has a reputation for being complicated—despite the ubiquity of strings, most programmers avoid learning about Unicode and hope for the best. But at a conceptual level, there's nothing to be afraid of. The basics of Unicode are perfectly simple: Every unit of text of all the world's writing systems is assigned a unique integer between 0 and 1,114,111, known as a *code point* in Unicode terminology. That's it—hardly any different from any other text encoding, such as

ASCII. The difference, however, is that while ASCII maps each index to a unique binary representation, Unicode allows multiple different binary encodings of code points. Different encodings make trade-offs between the amount of storage required for a string and the speed of operations such as indexing into a string. Today there are multiple standard encodings of Unicode, the most popular of which are UTF-8, UTF-16, and UTF-32.

Complicating the picture further, the designers of Unicode historically miscalculated their budget for code points. It was originally thought that Unicode would need no more than 2^{16} code points. This made UCS-2, the original standard 16-bit encoding, a particularly attractive choice. Since every code point could fit in a 16-bit number, there was a simple, one-to-one mapping between code points and the elements of their encodings, known as *code units.* That is, UCS-2 was made up of individual 16-bit code units, each of which corresponded to a single Unicode code point. The primary benefit of this encoding is that indexing into a string is a cheap, constant-time operation: Accessing the *n*th code point of a string simply selects from the *n*th 16-bit element of the array. Figure 1.1 shows an example string consisting only of code points in the original 16-bit range. As you can see, the indices match up perfectly between elements of the encoding and code points in the Unicode string.

As a result, a number of platforms at the time committed to using a 16-bit encoding of strings. Java was one such platform, and JavaScript followed suit: Every element of a JavaScript string is a 16-bit value. Now, if Unicode had remained as it was in the early 1990s, each element of a JavaScript string would still correspond to a single code point.

This 16-bit range is quite large, encompassing far more of the world's text systems than ASCII or any of its myriad historical successors ever did. Even so, in time it became clear that Unicode would outgrow

'h'	'e'	'l'	'l'	'o'
0x0068	0x0065	0x006c	0x006c	0x006f
0	1	2	3	4

Figure 1.1 A JavaScript string containing code points from the Basic Multilingual Plane

its initial range, and the standard expanded to its current range of over 2^{20} code points. The new increased range is organized into 17 subranges of 2^{16} code points each. The first of these, known as the *Basic Multilingual Plane* (or BMP), consists of the original 2^{16} code points. The additional 16 ranges are known as the *supplementary planes.*

Once the range of code points expanded, UCS-2 had become obsolete: It needed to be extended to represent the additional code points. Its successor, UTF-16, is mostly the same, but with the addition of what are known as *surrogate pairs:* pairs of 16-bit code units that together encode a single code point 2^{16} or greater. For example, the musical G clef symbol ("𝄞"), which is assigned the code point U+1D11E—the conventional hexadecimal spelling of code point number 119,070—is represented in UTF-16 by the pair of code units 0xd834 and 0xdd1e. The code point can be decoded by combining selected bits from each of the two code units. (Cleverly, the encoding ensures that neither of these "surrogates" can ever be confused for a valid BMP code point, so you can always tell if you're looking at a surrogate, even if you start searching from somewhere in the middle of a string.) You can see an example of a string with a surrogate pair in Figure 1.2. The first code point of the string requires a surrogate pair, causing the indices of code units to differ from the indices of code points.

Because each code point in a UTF-16 encoding may require either one or two 16-bit code units, UTF-16 is a *variable-length* encoding: The size in memory of a string of length *n* varies based on the particular code points in the string. Moreover, finding the *n*th code point of a string is no longer a constant-time operation: It generally requires searching from the beginning of the string.

But by the time Unicode expanded in size, JavaScript had already committed to 16-bit string elements. String properties and methods such as length, charAt, and charCodeAt all work at the level of code

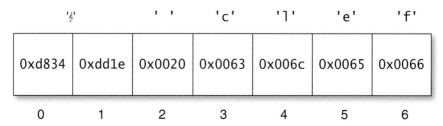

Figure 1.2 A JavaScript string containing a code point from a supplementary plane

units rather than code *points.* So whenever a string contains code points from the supplementary planes, JavaScript represents each as two elements—the code point's UTF-16 surrogate pair—rather than one. Simply put:

An element of a JavaScript string is a 16-bit code unit.

Internally, JavaScript engines may optimize the storage of string contents. But as far as their properties and methods are concerned, strings behave like sequences of UTF-16 code units. Consider the string from Figure 1.2. Despite the fact that the string contains six code points, JavaScript reports its length as 7:

```
"𝄞 clef".length; // 7
"G clef".length; // 6
```

Extracting individual elements of the string produces code units rather than code points:

```
"𝄞 clef".charCodeAt(0);      // 55348 (0xd834)
"𝄞 clef".charCodeAt(1);      // 56606 (0xdd1e)
"𝄞 clef".charAt(1) === " "; // false
"𝄞 clef".charAt(2) === " "; // true
```

Similarly, regular expressions operate at the level of code units. The single-character pattern (".") matches a single code unit:

```
/^.$/.test("𝄞");  // false
/^..$/.test("𝄞"); // true
```

This state of affairs means that applications working with the full range of Unicode have to work a lot harder: They can't rely on string methods, length values, indexed lookups, or many regular expression patterns. If you are working outside the BMP, it's a good idea to look for help from code point-aware libraries. It can be tricky to get the details of encoding and decoding right, so it's advisable to use an existing library rather than implement the logic yourself.

While JavaScript's built-in string datatype operates at the level of code units, this doesn't prevent APIs from being aware of code points and surrogate pairs. In fact, some of the standard ECMAScript libraries correctly handle surrogate pairs, such as the URI manipulation functions `encodeURI`, `decodeURI`, `encodeURIComponent`, and `decodeURIComponent`. Whenever a JavaScript environment provides a library that operates on strings—for example, manipulating the contents of a web page or performing I/O with strings—you should consult the library's documentation to see how it handles the full range of Unicode code points.

Things to Remember

✦ JavaScript strings consist of 16-bit code units, not Unicode code points.

✦ Unicode code points 2^{16} and above are represented in JavaScript by two code units, known as a surrogate pair.

✦ Surrogate pairs throw off string element counts, affecting `length`, `charAt`, `charCodeAt`, and regular expression patterns such as ".".

✦ Use third-party libraries for writing code point-aware string manipulation.

✦ Whenever you are using a library that works with strings, consult the documentation to see how it handles the full range of code points.

2

Variable Scope

Scope is like oxygen to a programmer. It's everywhere. You often don't even think about it. But when it gets polluted . . . you choke.

The good news is that JavaScript's core scoping rules are simple, well designed, and incredibly powerful. But there are exceptions. Working effectively with JavaScript requires mastering some basic concepts of variable scope as well as the corner cases that can lead to subtle but nasty problems.

Item 8: Minimize Use of the Global Object

JavaScript makes it easy to create variables in its global namespace. Global variables take less effort to create, since they don't require any kind of declaration, and they are automatically accessible to all code throughout the program. This convenience makes them an easy temptation for beginners. But seasoned programmers know to avoid global variables. Defining global variables pollutes the common namespace shared by everyone, introducing the possibility of accidental name collisions. Globals go against the grain of modularity: They lead to unnecessary coupling between separate components of a program. As convenient as it may be to "code now and organize later," the best programmers constantly pay attention to the structure of their programs, continuously grouping related functionality and separating unrelated components as a part of the programming process.

Since the global namespace is the only real way for separate components of a JavaScript program to interact, some uses of the global namespace are unavoidable. A component or library has to define a global name so that other parts of the program can use it. Otherwise, it's best to keep variables as local as possible. It's certainly *possible* to write a program with nothing but global variables, but it's asking for trouble. Even very simple functions that define their temporary variables globally would have to worry whether any other code might use those same variable names:

```
var i, n, sum; // globals
function averageScore(players) {
    sum = 0;
    for (i = 0, n = players.length; i < n; i++) {
        sum += score(players[i]);
    }
    return sum / n;
}
```

This definition of averageScore won't work if the score function it depends on uses any of the same global variables for its own purposes:

```
var i, n, sum; // same globals as averageScore!
function score(player) {
    sum = 0;
    for (i = 0, n = player.levels.length; i < n; i++) {
        sum += player.levels[i].score;
    }
    return sum;
}
```

The answer is to keep such variables local to just the portion of code that needs them:

```
function averageScore(players) {
    var i, n, sum;
    sum = 0;
    for (i = 0, n = players.length; i < n; i++) {
        sum += score(players[i]);
    }
    return sum / n;
}

function score(player) {
    var i, n, sum;
    sum = 0;
    for (i = 0, n = player.levels.length; i < n; i++) {
        sum += player.levels[i].score;
    }
    return sum;
}
```

JavaScript's global namespace is also exposed as a *global object*, which is accessible at the top of a program as the initial value of the this keyword. In web browsers, the global object is also bound to the global `window` variable. Adding or modifying global variables automatically updates the global object:

```
this.foo; // undefined
foo = "global foo";
this.foo; // "global foo"
```

Similarly, updating the global object automatically updates the global namespace:

```
var foo = "global foo";
this.foo = "changed";
foo; // "changed"
```

This means that you have two mechanisms to choose from for creating a global variable: You can declare it with var in the global scope, or you can add it to the global object. Either works, but the var declaration has the benefit of more clearly conveying the effect on the program's scope. Given that a reference to an unbound variable results in a runtime error, making scope clear and simple makes it easier for users of your code to understand what globals it declares.

While it's best to limit your use of the global object, it does provide one particularly indispensable use. Since the global object provides a dynamic reflection of the global environment, you can use it to query a running environment to detect which features are available on the platform. For example, ES5 introduced a new global JSON object for reading and writing the JSON data format. As a stopgap for deploying code in environments that may or may not have yet provided the JSON object, you can test the global object for its presence and provide an alternate implementation:

```
if (!this.JSON) {
    this.JSON = {
        parse: ...,
        stringify: ...
    };
}
```

If you are already providing an implementation of JSON, you could of course simply use your own implementation unconditionally. But built-in implementations provided by the host environment are almost always preferable: They are highly tested for correctness and conformance to standards, and quite often provide better performance than a third-party implementation.

The technique of feature detection is especially important in web browsers, where the same code may be executed by a wide variety of browsers and browser versions. Feature detection is a relatively easy way to make programs robust to the variations in platform feature sets. The technique applies elsewhere, too, such as for sharing libraries that may work both in the browser and in JavaScript server environments.

Things to Remember

✦ Avoid declaring global variables.

✦ Declare variables as locally as possible.

✦ Avoid adding properties to the global object.

✦ Use the global object for platform feature detection.

Item 9: Always Declare Local Variables

If there's one thing more troublesome than a global variable, it's an *unintentional* global variable. Unfortunately, JavaScript's variable assignment rules make it all too easy to create global variables accidentally. Instead of raising an error, a program that assigns to an unbound variable simply creates a new global variable and assigns to it. This means that forgetting to declare a local variable silently turns it into a global variable:

```
function swap(a, i, j) {
    temp = a[i]; // global
    a[i] = a[j];
    a[j] = temp;
}
```

This program manages to execute without error, even though the lack of a var declaration for the temp variable leads to the accidental creation of a global variable. A proper implementation declares temp with var:

```
function swap(a, i, j) {
    var temp = a[i];
    a[i] = a[j];
    a[j] = temp;
}
```

Purposefully creating global variables is bad style, but accidentally creating global variables can be a downright disaster. Because of this, many programmers use *lint* tools, which inspect your program's source code for bad style or potential bugs, and often feature the ability to report uses of unbound variables. Typically, a lint tool that checks for undeclared variables takes a user-provided set of known globals (such as those expected to exist in the host environment, or globals defined in separate files) and then reports any references or assignments to variables that are neither provided in the list nor declared in the program. It's worth taking some time to explore what development tools are available for JavaScript. Integrating automated checks for common errors such as accidental globals into your development process can be a lifesaver.

Things to Remember

✦ Always declare new local variables with var.

✦ Consider using lint tools to help check for unbound variables.

Item 10: Avoid with

Poor with. There is probably no single more maligned feature in JavaScript. Nevertheless, with came by its notoriety honestly: Whatever conveniences it may offer, it more than makes up for them in unreliability and inefficiency.

The motivations for with are understandable. Programs often need to call a number of methods in sequence on a single object, and it is convenient to avoid repeated references to the object:

```
function status(info) {
    var widget = new Widget();
    with (widget) {
        setBackground("blue");
        setForeground("white");
        setText("Status: " + info); // ambiguous reference
        show();
    }
}
```

It's also tempting to use with to "import" variables from objects serving as modules:

```
function f(x, y) {
    with (Math) {
        return min(round(x), sqrt(y)); // ambiguous references
    }
}
```

In both cases, with makes it temptingly easy to extract the properties of an object and bind them as local variables in the block.

These examples look appealing. But neither actually does what it's supposed to. Notice how both examples have two different kinds of variables: those that we expect to refer to properties of the with object, such as setBackground, round, and sqrt, and those that we expect to refer to outer variable bindings, such as info, x, and y. But nothing in the syntax actually distinguishes these two types of variables—they all just look like variables.

In fact, JavaScript treats all variables the same: It looks them up in scope, starting with the innermost scope and working its way outward. The with statement treats an object as if it represented a variable scope, so inside the with block, variable lookup starts by searching for a property of the given variable name. If the property is not found in the object, then the search continues in outer scopes.

Figure 2.1 shows a diagram of a JavaScript engine's internal representation of the scope of the status function while executing the body of its with statement. This is known in the ES5 specification as the *lexical environment* (or *scope chain* in older versions of the standard). The innermost scope of the environment is provided by the widget object. The next scope out has bindings for the function's local variables info and widget. At the next level is a binding for the status function. Notice how, in a normal scope, there are exactly as many bindings stored in that level of the environment as there are variables in that local scope. But for the with scope, the set of bindings is dependent on whatever happens to be in the object at a given point in time.

How confident are we that we know what properties will or won't be found on the object we provided to with? Every reference to an outer variable in a with block implicitly assumes that there is no property of the same name in the with object—*or in any of its prototype objects.* Other parts of the program that create or modify the with object and its prototypes may not share those assumptions. They certainly should not have to read your local code to find what local variables you happen to be using.

This conflict between variable scope and object namespaces makes with blocks extremely brittle. For example, if the widget object in the above example acquires an info property, then suddenly the behavior of the status function will use that property instead of the status function's info parameter. This could happen during the evolution of the source code if, for example, a programmer decides that all widgets

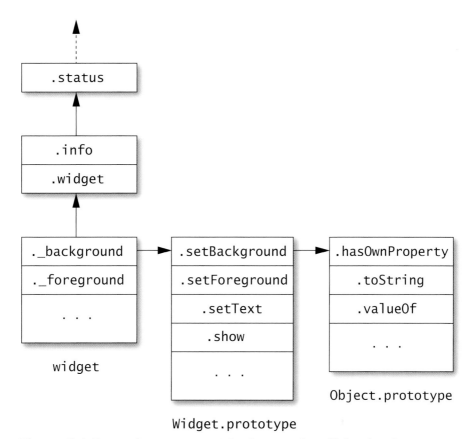

Figure 2.1 Lexical environment (or "scope chain") for the status function

should have an info property. Worse, something could add an info property to the Widget prototype object at runtime, causing the status function to start breaking at unpredictable points:

```
status("connecting"); // Status: connecting
Widget.prototype.info = "[[widget info]]";
status("connected");  // Status: [[widget info]]
```

Similarly, the function f above could be broken if someone adds an x or y property to the Math object:

```
Math.x = 0;
Math.y = 0;
f(2, 9); // 0
```

It might be unlikely that anyone would add x and y properties to Math. But it's not always easy to predict whether a particular object might be modified, or might have properties you didn't know about. And as it turns out, a feature that is unpredictable for humans can also be unpredictable for optimizing compilers. Normally, JavaScript scopes can be represented with efficient internal data structures and variable lookups can be performed quickly. But because a with block requires searching an object's prototype chain for *all* variables in its body, it will typically run much more slowly than an ordinary block.

There is no single feature of JavaScript that directly replaces with as a better alternative. In some cases, the best alternative is simply to bind an object to a short variable name:

```
function status(info) {
    var w = new Widget();
    w.setBackground("blue");
    w.setForeground("white");
    w.addText("Status: " + info);
    w.show();
}
```

The behavior of this version is much more predictable. None of the variable references are sensitive to the contents of the object w. So even if some code modifies the Widget prototype, status continues to behave as expected:

```
status("connecting"); // Status: connecting
Widget.prototype.info = "[[widget info]]";
status("connected");  // Status: connected
```

In other cases, the best approach is to bind local variables explicitly to the relevant properties:

```
function f(x, y) {
    var min = Math.min, round = Math.round, sqrt = Math.sqrt;
    return min(round(x), sqrt(y));
}
```

Again, once we eliminate with, the function's behavior becomes predictable:

```
Math.x = 0;
Math.y = 0;
f(2, 9); // 2
```

Things to Remember

✦ Avoid using `with` statements.

✦ Use short variable names for repeated access to an object.

✦ Explicitly bind local variables to object properties instead of implicitly binding them with a `with` statement.

Item 11: Get Comfortable with Closures

Closures may be an unfamiliar concept to programmers coming from languages that don't support them. And they may seem intimidating at first. But rest assured that making the effort to master closures will pay for itself many times over.

Luckily, there's really nothing to be afraid of. Understanding closures only requires learning three essential facts. The first fact is that JavaScript allows you to refer to variables that were defined outside of the current function:

```
function makeSandwich() {
    var magicIngredient = "peanut butter";
    function make(filling) {
        return magicIngredient + " and " + filling;
    }
    return make("jelly");
}
makeSandwich(); // "peanut butter and jelly"
```

Notice how the inner `make` function refers to `magicIngredient`, a variable defined in the outer `makeSandwich` function.

The second fact is that functions can refer to variables defined in outer functions even *after* those outer functions have returned! If that sounds implausible, remember that JavaScript functions are first-class objects (see Item 19). That means that you can return an inner function to be called sometime later on:

```
function sandwichMaker() {
    var magicIngredient = "peanut butter";
    function make(filling) {
        return magicIngredient + " and " + filling;
    }
    return make;
}
var f = sandwichMaker();
f("jelly");          // "peanut butter and jelly"
```

```
f("bananas");       // "peanut butter and bananas"
f("marshmallows"); // "peanut butter and marshmallows"
```

This is almost identical to the first example, except that instead of immediately calling make("jelly") inside the outer function, sandwichMaker returns the make function itself. So the value of f is the inner make function, and calling f effectively calls make. But somehow, even though sandwichMaker already returned, make remembers the value of magicIngredient.

How does this work? The answer is that JavaScript function values contain more information than just the code required to execute when they're called. They also internally store any variables they may refer to that are defined in their enclosing scopes. Functions that keep track of variables from their containing scopes are known as *closures*. The make function is a closure whose code refers to two outer variables: magicIngredient and filling. Whenever the make function is called, its code is able to refer to these two variables because they are stored in the closure.

A function can refer to any variables in its scope, including the parameters and variables of outer functions. We can use this to make a more general-purpose sandwichMaker:

```
function sandwichMaker(magicIngredient) {
    function make(filling) {
        return magicIngredient + " and " + filling;
    }
    return make;
}
var hamAnd = sandwichMaker("ham");
hamAnd("cheese");        // "ham and cheese"
hamAnd("mustard");       // "ham and mustard"
var turkeyAnd = sandwichMaker("turkey");
turkeyAnd("Swiss");      // "turkey and Swiss"
turkeyAnd("Provolone");  // "turkey and Provolone"
```

This example creates two distinct functions, hamAnd and turkeyAnd. Even though they both come from the same make definition, they are two distinct objects: The first function stores "ham" as the value of magicIngredient, and the second stores "turkey".

Closures are one of JavaScript's most elegant and expressive features, and are at the heart of many useful idioms. JavaScript even provides a more convenient literal syntax for constructing closures, the *function expression:*

```
function sandwichMaker(magicIngredient) {
    return function(filling) {
        return magicIngredient + " and " + filling;
    };
}
```

Notice that this function expression is anonymous: It's not even necessary to name the function since we are only evaluating it to produce a new function value, but do not intend to call it locally. Function expressions can have names as well (see Item 14).

The third and final fact to learn about closures is that they can update the values of outer variables. Closures actually store *references* to their outer variables, rather than copying their values. So updates are visible to any closures that have access to them. A simple idiom that illustrates this is a *box*—an object that stores an internal value that can be read and updated:

```
function box() {
    var val = undefined;
    return {
        set: function(newVal) { val = newVal; },
        get: function() { return val; },
        type: function() { return typeof val; }
    };
}
var b = box();
b.type(); // "undefined"
b.set(98.6);
b.get();  // 98.6
b.type(); // "number"
```

This example produces an object containing three closures: its set, get, and type properties. Each of these closures shares access to the val variable. The set closure updates the value of val, and subsequently calling get and type sees the results of the update.

Things to Remember

◆ Functions can refer to variables defined in outer scopes.

◆ Closures can outlive the function that creates them.

◆ Closures internally store references to their outer variables, and can both read and update their stored variables.

Item 12: Understand Variable Hoisting

JavaScript supports *lexical scoping:* With only a few exceptions, a reference to a variable foo is bound to the nearest scope in which foo was declared. However, JavaScript does not support *block scoping:* Variable definitions are not scoped to their nearest enclosing statement or block, but rather to their containing function.

Failing to understand this idiosyncrasy of JavaScript can lead to subtle bugs such as this:

```
function isWinner(player, others) {
    var highest = 0;
    for (var i = 0, n = others.length; i < n; i++) {
        var player = others[i];
        if (player.score > highest) {
            highest = player.score;
        }
    }
    return player.score > highest;
}
```

This program appears to declare a local variable player within the body of a for loop. But because JavaScript variables are function-scoped rather than block-scoped, the inner declaration of player simply redeclares a variable that was already in scope—namely, the player parameter. Each iteration of the loop then overwrites the same variable. As a result, the return statement sees player as the last element of others instead of the function's original player argument.

A good way to think about the behavior of JavaScript variable declarations is to understand them as consisting of two parts: a declaration and an assignment. JavaScript implicitly "hoists" the declaration part to the top of the enclosing function and leaves the assignment in place. In other words, the variable is in scope for the entire function, but it is only assigned at the point where the var statement appears. Figure 2.2 provides a visualization of hoisting.

Hoisting can also lead to confusion about variable redeclaration. It is legal to declare the same variable multiple times within the same function. This often comes up when writing multiple loops:

```
function trimSections(header, body, footer) {
    for (var i = 0, n = header.length; i < n; i++) {
        header[i] = header[i].trim();
    }
```

```
    for (var i = 0, n = body.length; i < n; i++) {
        body[i] = body[i].trim();
    }
    for (var i = 0, n = footer.length; i < n; i++) {
        footer[i] = footer[i].trim();
    }
}
```

The `trimSections` function appears to declare six local variables (three called i and three called n), but hoisting results in only two. In other words, after hoisting, the `trimSections` function is equivalent to this rewritten version:

```
function trimSections(header, body, footer) {
    var i, n;
    for (i = 0, n = header.length; i < n; i++) {
        header[i] = header[i].trim();
    }
    for (i = 0, n = body.length; i < n; i++) {
        body[i] = body[i].trim();
    }
    for (i = 0, n = footer.length; i < n; i++) {
        footer[i] = footer[i].trim();
    }
}
```

Because redeclarations can lead to the appearance of distinct variables, some programmers prefer to place all var declarations at the top of their functions, effectively hoisting their variables manually, in order to avoid ambiguity. Regardless of whether you prefer this style, it's important to understand the scoping rules of JavaScript, both for writing and reading code.

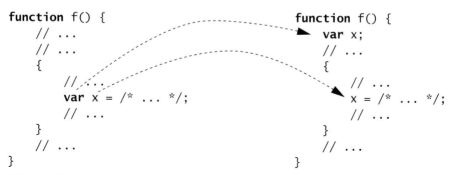

Figure 2.2 Variable hoisting

The one exception to JavaScript's lack of block scoping is, appropriately enough, exceptions. That is, try...catch binds a caught exception to a variable that is scoped just to the catch block:

```
function test() {
    var x = "var", result = [];
    result.push(x);
    try {
        throw "exception";
    } catch (x) {
        x = "catch";
    }
    result.push(x);
    return result;
}
test(); // ["var", "var"]
```

Things to Remember

✦ Variable declarations within a block are implicitly hoisted to the top of their enclosing function.

✦ Redeclarations of a variable are treated as a single variable.

✦ Consider manually hoisting local variable declarations to avoid confusion.

Item 13: Use Immediately Invoked Function Expressions to Create Local Scopes

What does this (buggy!) program compute?

```
function wrapElements(a) {
    var result = [], i, n;
    for (i = 0, n = a.length; i < n; i++) {
        result[i] = function() { return a[i]; };
    }
    return result;
}

var wrapped = wrapElements([10, 20, 30, 40, 50]);
var f = wrapped[0];
f(); // ?
```

The programmer may have intended for it to produce 10, but it actually produces the undefined value.

The way to make sense of this example is to understand the distinction between binding and assignment. Entering a scope at runtime allocates a "slot" in memory for each variable binding in that scope. The wrapElements function binds three local variables: result, i, and n. So when it is called, wrapElements allocates slots for these three variables. On each iteration of the loop, the loop body allocates a closure for the nested function. The bug in the program comes from the fact that the programmer apparently expected the function to store the value of i at the time the nested function was created. But in fact, it contains a *reference* to i. Since the value of i changes after each function is created, the inner functions end up seeing the final value of i. This is the key point about closures:

Closures store their outer variables by reference, not by value.

So all the closures created by wrapElements refer to the single shared slot for i that was created before the loop. Since each iteration of the loop increments i until it runs off the end of the array, by the time we actually call one of the closures, it looks up index 5 of the array and returns undefined.

Notice that wrapElements would behave exactly the same even if we put the var declarations in the head of the for loop:

```
function wrapElements(a) {
    var result = [];
    for (var i = 0, n = a.length; i < n; i++) {
        result[i] = function() { return a[i]; };
    }
    return result;
}

var wrapped = wrapElements([10, 20, 30, 40, 50]);
var f = wrapped[0];
f(); // undefined
```

This version looks even a bit more deceptive, because the var declaration appears to be inside the loop. But as always, the variable declarations are hoisted to the top of the loop. So once again, there is only a single slot allocated for the variable i.

The solution is to force the creation of a local scope by creating a nested function and calling it right away:

```
function wrapElements(a) {
    var result = [];
    for (var i = 0, n = a.length; i < n; i++) {
```

```
        (function() {
            var j = i;
            result[i] = function() { return a[j]; };
        })();
    }
    return result;
}
```

This technique, known as the *immediately invoked function expression*, or IIFE (pronounced "iffy"), is an indispensable workaround for JavaScript's lack of block scoping. An alternate variation is to bind the local variable as a parameter to the IIFE and pass its value as an argument:

```
function wrapElements(a) {
    var result = [];
    for (var i = 0, n = a.length; i < n; i++) {
        (function(j) {
            result[i] = function() { return a[j]; };
        })(i);
    }
    return result;
}
```

However, be careful when using an IIFE to create a local scope, because wrapping a block in a function can introduce some subtle changes to the block. First of all, the block cannot contain any break or continue statements that jump outside of the block, since it is illegal to break or continue outside of a function. Second, if the block refers to this or the special arguments variable, the IIFE changes their meaning. Chapter 3 discusses techniques for working with this and arguments.

Things to Remember

✦ Understand the difference between binding and assignment.

✦ Closures capture their outer variables by reference, not by value.

✦ Use immediately invoked function expressions (IIFEs) to create local scopes.

✦ Be aware of the cases where wrapping a block in an IIFE can change its behavior.

Item 14: Beware of Unportable Scoping of Named Function Expressions

JavaScript functions may look the same wherever they go, but their meaning changes depending on the context. Take a code snippet such as the following:

```
function double(x) { return x * 2; }
```

Depending on where it appears, this could be either a *function declaration* or a *named function expression*. A declaration is familiar: It defines a function and binds it to a variable in the current scope. At the top level of a program, for example, the above declaration would create a global function called double. But the same function code can be used as an expression, where it has a very different meaning. For example:

```
var f = function double(x) { return x * 2; };
```

According to the ECMAScript specification, this binds the function to a variable f rather than double. Of course, we don't have to give a function expression a name. We could use the anonymous function expression form:

```
var f = function(x) { return x * 2; };
```

The official difference between anonymous and named function expressions is that the latter binds its name as a local variable within the function. This can be used to write recursive function expressions:

```
var f = function find(tree, key) {
    if (!tree) {
        return null;
    }
    if (tree.key === key) {
        return tree.value;
    }
    return find(tree.left, key) ||
            find(tree.right, key);
};
```

Note that find is only in scope within the function itself. Unlike a function declaration, a named function expression can't be referred to externally by its internal name:

```
find(myTree, "foo"); // error: find is not defined
```

Using named function expressions for recursion may not seem particularly useful, since it's fine to use the outer scope's name for the function:

```
var f = function(tree, key) {
    if (!tree) {
        return null;
    }
    if (tree.key === key) {
        return tree.value;
    }
    return f(tree.left, key) ||
           f(tree.right, key);
};
```

Or we could just use a declaration:

```
function find(tree, key) {
    if (!tree) {
        return null;
    }
    if (tree.key === key) {
        return tree.value;
    }
    return find(tree.left, key) ||
           find(tree.right, key);
}
var f = find;
```

The real usefulness of named function expressions, though, is for debugging. Most modern JavaScript environments produce stack traces for Error objects, and the name of a function expression is typically used for its entry in a stack trace. Debuggers with facilities for inspecting the stack typically make similar use of named function expressions.

Sadly, named function expressions have been a notorious source of scoping and compatibility issues, due to a combination of an unfortunate mistake in the history of the ECMAScript specification and bugs in popular JavaScript engines. The specification mistake, which existed through ES3, was that JavaScript engines were required to represent the scope of a named function expression as an object, much like the problematic with construct. While this scope object only contains a single property binding the function's name to the function, it also inherits properties from Object.prototype. This means that just naming a function expression also brings all of the properties of Object.prototype into scope. The results can be surprising:

```
var constructor = function() { return null; };
var f = function f() {
    return constructor();
};
f(); // {} (in ES3 environments)
```

This program looks like it should produce null, but it actually produces a new object, because the named function expression inherits Object.prototype.constructor (i.e., the Object constructor function) in its scope. And just like with, the scope is affected by dynamic changes to Object.prototype. One part of a program could add or delete properties to Object.prototype and variables within named function expressions everywhere would be affected.

Thankfully, ES5 corrected this mistake. But some JavaScript environments continue to use the obsolete object scoping. Worse, some are even less standards-compliant and use objects as scopes *even for anonymous function expressions!* Then, even removing the function expression's name in the preceding example produces an object instead of the expected null:

```
var constructor = function() { return null; };
var f = function() {
    return constructor();
};
f(); // {} (in nonconformant environments)
```

The best way to avoid these problems on systems that pollute their function expressions' scopes with objects is to avoid ever adding new properties to Object.prototype and avoid using local variables with any of the names of the standard Object.prototype properties.

The next bug seen in popular JavaScript engines is hoisting named function expressions as if they were declarations. For example:

```
var f = function g() { return 17; };
g(); // 17 (in nonconformant environments)
```

To be clear, this is *not* standards-compliant behavior. Worse, some JavaScript environments even treat the two functions f and g as distinct objects, leading to unnecessary memory allocation! A reasonable workaround for this behavior is to create a local variable of the same name as the function expression and assign it to null:

```
var f = function g() { return 17; };
var g = null;
```

Redeclaring the variable with var ensures that g is bound even in those environments that do not erroneously hoist the function expression, and setting it to `null` ensures that the duplicate function can be garbage-collected.

It would certainly be reasonable to conclude that named function expressions are just too problematic to be worth using. A less austere response would be to use named function expressions during development for debugging, and to run code through a preprocessor to anonymize all function expressions before shipping. But one thing is certain: You should always be clear about what platforms you are shipping on (see Item 1). The worst thing you could do is to litter your code with workarounds that aren't even necessary for the platforms you support.

Things to Remember

✦ Use named function expressions to improve stack traces in `Error` objects and debuggers.

✦ Beware of pollution of function expression scope with `Object` `.prototype` in ES3 and buggy JavaScript environments.

✦ Beware of hoisting and duplicate allocation of named function expressions in buggy JavaScript environments.

✦ Consider avoiding named function expressions or removing them before shipping.

✦ If you are shipping in properly implemented ES5 environments, you've got nothing to worry about.

Item 15: Beware of Unportable Scoping of Block-Local Function Declarations

The saga of context sensitivity continues with nested function declarations. It may surprise you to know that there is no standard way to declare functions inside a local block. Now, it's perfectly legal and customary to nest a function declaration at the top of another function:

```
function f() { return "global"; }

function test(x) {
    function f() { return "local"; }

    var result = [];
    if (x) {
        result.push(f());
    }
```

```
        result.push(f());
        return result;
}

test(true);  // ["local", "local"]
test(false); // ["local"]
```

But it's an entirely different story if we move f into a local block:

```
function f() { return "global"; }

function test(x) {
    var result = [];
    if (x) {
        function f() { return "local"; } // block-local

        result.push(f());
    }
    result.push(f());
    return result;
}

test(true);  // ?
test(false); // ?
```

You might expect the first call to test to produce the array ["local", "global"] and the second to produce ["global"], since the inner f appears to be local to the if block. But recall that JavaScript is not block-scoped, so the inner f should be in scope for the whole body of test. A reasonable second guess would be ["local", "local"] and ["local"]. And in fact, some JavaScript environments behave this way. But not all of them! Others *conditionally* bind the inner f at runtime, based on whether its enclosing block is executed. (Not only does this make code harder to understand, but it also leads to slow performance, not unlike with statements.)

What does the ECMAScript standard have to say about this state of affairs? Surprisingly, almost nothing. Until ES5, the standard did not even acknowledge the existence of block-local function declarations; function declarations are officially specified to appear only at the outermost level of other functions or of a program. ES5 even recommends turning function declarations in nonstandard contexts into a warning or error, and popular JavaScript implementations report them as an error in strict mode—a strict-mode program with a block-local function declaration will report a syntax error. This helps detect unportable code, and it clears a path for future versions of the standard to specify more sensible and portable semantics for block-local declarations.

In the meantime, the best way to write portable functions is to avoid ever putting function declarations in local blocks or substatements. If you want to write a nested function declaration, put it at the outer-most level of its parent function, as shown in the original version of the code. If, on the other hand, you need to choose between functions conditionally, the best way to do this is with var declarations and function expressions:

```
function f() { return "global"; }

function test(x) {
    var g = f, result = [];
    if (x) {
        g = function() { return "local"; }

        result.push(g());
    }
    result.push(g());
    return result;
}
```

This eliminates the mystery of the scoping of the inner variable (renamed here to g): It is unconditionally bound as a local variable, and only the assignment is conditional. The result is unambiguous and fully portable.

Things to Remember

✦ Always keep function declarations at the outermost level of a program or a containing function to avoid unportable behavior.

✦ Use var declarations with conditional assignment instead of conditional function declarations.

Item 16: Avoid Creating Local Variables with eval

JavaScript's eval function is an incredibly powerful and flexible tool. Powerful tools are easy to abuse, so they're worth understanding. One of the simplest ways to run afoul of eval is to allow it to interfere with scope.

Calling eval interprets its argument as a JavaScript program, but that program runs in the local scope of the caller. The global variables of the embedded program get created as locals of the calling program:

```
function test(x) {
    eval("var y = x;"); // dynamic binding
    return y;
}
test("hello"); // "hello"
```

This example looks clear, but it behaves subtly differently than the var declaration would behave if it were directly included in the body of test. The var declaration is only executed when the eval function is called. Placing an eval in a conditional context brings its variables into scope only if the conditional is executed:

```
var y = "global";
function test(x) {
    if (x) {
        eval("var y = 'local';"); // dynamic binding
    }
    return y;
}
test(true);  // "local"
test(false); // "global"
```

Basing scoping decisions on the dynamic behavior of a program is almost always a bad idea. The result is that simply understanding which binding a variable refers to requires following the details of how the program executes. This is especially tricky when the source code passed to eval is not even defined locally:

```
var y = "global";
function test(src) {
    eval(src); // may dynamically bind
    return y;
}
test("var y = 'local';"); // "local"
test("var z = 'local';"); // "global"
```

This code is brittle and unsafe: It gives external callers the power to change the internal scoping of the test function. Expecting eval to modify its containing scope is also not safe for compatibility with ES5 strict mode, which runs eval in a nested scope to prevent this kind of pollution. A simple way to ensure that eval does not affect outer scopes is to run it in an explicitly nested scope:

```
var y = "global";
function test(src) {
    (function() { eval(src); })();
    return y;
}
```

```
test("var y = 'local';"); // "global"
test("var z = 'local';"); // "global"
```

Things to Remember

+ Avoid creating variables with eval that pollute the caller's scope.

+ If eval code might create global variables, wrap the call in a nested function to prevent scope pollution.

Item 17: Prefer Indirect eval to Direct eval

The eval function has a secret weapon: It's more than just a function.

Most functions have access to the scope where they are defined, and nothing else. But eval has access to the full scope *at the point where it's called.* This is such immense power that when compiler writers first tried to optimize JavaScript, they discovered that eval made it difficult to make any function calls efficient, since every function call needed to make its scope available at runtime in case the function turned out to be eval.

As a compromise, the language standard evolved to distinguish two different ways of calling eval. A function call involving the identifier eval is considered a "direct" call to eval:

```
var x = "global";
function test() {
    var x = "local";
    return eval("x"); // direct eval
}
test(); // "local"
```

In this case, compilers are required to ensure that the executed program has complete access to the local scope of the caller. The other kind of call to eval is considered "indirect," and evaluates its argument in global scope. For example, binding the eval function to a different variable name and calling it through the alternate name causes the code to lose access to any local scope:

```
var x = "global";
function test() {
    var x = "local";
    var f = eval;
    return f("x"); // indirect eval
}
test(); // "global"
```

The exact definition of direct eval depends on the rather idiosyncratic specification language of the ECMAScript standard. In practice, the only syntax that can produce a direct eval is a variable with the name eval, possibly surrounded by (any number of) parentheses. A concise way to write an indirect call to eval is to use the expression sequencing operator (,) with an apparently pointless number literal:

```
(0,eval)(src);
```

How does this peculiar-looking function call work? The number literal 0 is evaluated but its value is ignored, and the parenthesized sequence expression produces the eval function. So (0,eval) behaves almost exactly the same as the plain identifier eval, with the one important difference being that the whole call expression is treated as an indirect eval.

The power of direct eval can be easily abused. For example, evaluating a source string coming from over the network can expose internals to untrusted parties. Item 16 talks about the dangers of eval dynamically creating local variables; these dangers are only possible with direct eval. Moreover, direct eval costs dearly in performance. In general, you should assume that direct eval causes its containing function and *all containing functions up to the outermost level of the program* to be considerably slower.

There are occasionally reasons to use direct eval. But unless there's a clear need for the extra power of inspecting local scope, use the less easily abused and less expensive indirect eval.

Things to Remember

✦ Wrap eval in a sequence expression with a useless literal to force the use of indirect eval.

✦ Prefer indirect eval to direct eval whenever possible.

3

Working with Functions

Functions are JavaScript's workhorse, serving simultaneously as the programmer's primary abstraction facility and implementation mechanism. Functions alone play roles that other languages fulfill with multiple distinct features: procedures, methods, constructors, and even classes and modules. Once you become comfortable with the finer points of functions, you have mastered a significant portion of JavaScript. The flip side of the coin is that it can take some time to learn how to use functions effectively in different contexts.

Item 18: Understand the Difference between Function, Method, and Constructor Calls

If you're familiar with object-oriented programming, you're likely accustomed to thinking of functions, methods, and class constructors as three separate things. In JavaScript, these are just three different usage patterns of one single construct: functions.

The simplest usage pattern is the function call:

```
function hello(username) {
    return "hello, " + username;
}
hello("Keyser Söze"); // "hello, Keyser Söze"
```

This does exactly what it looks like: It calls the `hello` function and binds the `username` parameter to its given argument.

Methods in JavaScript are nothing more than object properties that happen to be functions:

```
var obj = {
    hello: function() {
        return "hello, " + this.username;
    },
```

```
    username: "Hans Gruber"
};
obj.hello(); // "hello, Hans Gruber"
```

Notice how hello refers to this to access the properties of obj. You might be tempted to assume that this gets bound to obj because the hello method was defined on obj. But we can copy a reference to the same function in another object and get a different answer:

```
var obj2 = {
    hello: obj.hello,
    username: "Boo Radley"
};
obj2.hello(); // "hello, Boo Radley"
```

What really happens in a method call is that the call expression itself determines the binding of this, also known as the call's *receiver*. The expression obj.hello() looks up the hello property of obj and calls it with receiver obj. The expression obj2.hello() looks up the hello property of obj2—which happens to be the same function as obj.hello—but calls it with receiver obj2. In general, calling a method on an object looks up the method and then uses the object as the method's receiver.

Since methods are nothing more than functions called on a particular object, there is no reason why an ordinary function can't refer to this:

```
function hello() {
    return "hello, " + this.username;
}
```

This can be useful for predefining a function for sharing among multiple objects:

```
var obj1 = {
    hello: hello,
    username: "Gordon Gekko"
};
obj1.hello(); // "hello, Gordon Gekko"

var obj2 = {
    hello: hello,
    username: "Biff Tannen"
};
obj2.hello(); // "hello, Biff Tannen"
```

However, a function that uses this is not particularly useful to call as a function rather than a method:

`hello();` *// "hello, undefined"*

Rather unhelpfully, a nonmethod function call provides the global object as the receiver, which in this case has no property called `username` and produces `undefined`. Calling a method as a function rarely does anything useful if the method depends on `this`, since there is no reason to expect the global object to match the expectations that the method has of the object it is called on. In fact, binding to the global object is a problematic enough default that ES5's strict mode changes the default binding of `this` to `undefined`:

```
function hello() {
    "use strict";
    return "hello, " + this.username;
}
hello(); // error: cannot read property "username" of undefined
```

This helps catch accidental misuse of methods as plain functions by failing more quickly, since attempting to access properties of `undefined` immediately throws an error.

The third use of functions is as constructors. Just like methods and plain functions, constructors are defined with `function`:

```
function User(name, passwordHash) {
    this.name = name;
    this.passwordHash = passwordHash;
}
```

Invoking `User` with the `new` operator treats it as a constructor:

```
var u = new User("sfalken",
                 "0ef33ae791068ec64b502d6cb0191387");
u.name; // "sfalken"
```

Unlike function calls and method calls, a constructor call passes a brand-new object as the value of `this`, and implicitly returns the new object as its result. The constructor function's primary role is to initialize the object.

Things to Remember

✦ Method calls provide the object in which the method property is looked up as their receiver.

✦ Function calls provide the global object (or `undefined` for strict functions) as their receiver. Calling methods with function call syntax is rarely useful.

✦ Constructors are called with `new` and receive a fresh object as their receiver.

Item 19: Get Comfortable Using Higher-Order Functions

Higher-order functions used to be a shibboleth of the monks of functional programming, an esoteric term for what seemed like an advanced programming technique. Nothing could be further from the truth. Exploiting the concise elegance of functions can often lead to simpler and more succinct code. Over the years, scripting languages have adopted these techniques and in the process taken much of the mystery out of some of the best idioms of functional programming.

Higher-order functions are nothing more than functions that take other functions as arguments or return functions as their result. Taking a function as an argument (often referred to as a *callback function* because it is "called back" by the higher-order function) is a particularly powerful and expressive idiom, and one that JavaScript programs use heavily.

Consider the standard sort method on arrays. In order to work on all possible arrays, the sort method relies on the caller to determine how to compare any two elements in an array:

```
function compareNumbers(x, y) {
    if (x < y) {
        return -1;
    }
    if (x > y) {
        return 1;
    }
    return 0;
}
[3, 1, 4, 1, 5, 9].sort(compareNumbers); // [1, 1, 3, 4, 5, 9]
```

The standard library could have required the caller to pass in an object with a compare method, but since only one method is required, taking a function directly is simpler and more concise. In fact, the above example can be simplified further with an anonymous function:

```
[3, 1, 4, 1, 5, 9].sort(function(x, y) {
    if (x < y) {
        return -1;
    }
    if (x > y) {
        return 1;
    }
    return 0;
}); // [1, 1, 3, 4, 5, 9]
```

Learning to use higher-order functions can often simplify your code and eliminate tedious boilerplate. Many common operations on arrays have lovely higher-order abstractions that are worth familiarizing yourself with. Consider the simple act of transforming an array of strings. With a loop, we'd write:

```
var names = ["Fred", "Wilma", "Pebbles"];
var upper = [];
for (var i = 0, n = names.length; i < n; i++) {
    upper[i] = names[i].toUpperCase();
}
upper; // ["FRED", "WILMA", "PEBBLES"]
```

With the handy map method of arrays (introduced in ES5), we can completely eliminate the loop details, implementing just the element-by-element transformation with a local function:

```
var names = ["Fred", "Wilma", "Pebbles"];
var upper = names.map(function(name) {
    return name.toUpperCase();
});
upper; // ["FRED", "WILMA", "PEBBLES"]
```

Once you get the hang of using higher-order functions, you can start identifying opportunities to write your own. The telltale sign of a higher-order abstraction waiting to happen is duplicate or similar code. For example, imagine we found one part of a program constructing a string with the letters of the alphabet:

```
var aIndex = "a".charCodeAt(0); // 97

var alphabet = "";
for (var i = 0; i < 26; i++) {
    alphabet += String.fromCharCode(aIndex + i);
}
alphabet; // "abcdefghijklmnopqrstuvwxyz"
```

Meanwhile, another part of the program generates a string containing numeric digits:

```
var digits = "";
for (var i = 0; i < 10; i++) {
    digits += i;
}
digits; // "0123456789"
```

Still elsewhere, the program creates a random string of characters:

```
var random = "";

for (var i = 0; i < 8; i++) {
    random += String.fromCharCode(Math.floor(Math.random() * 26)
                                  + aIndex);
}
random; // "bdwvfrtp" (different result each time)
```

Each example creates a different string, but they all share common logic. Each loop creates a string by concatenating the results of some computation to create each individual segment. We can extract the common parts and move them into a single utility function:

```
function buildString(n, callback) {
    var result = "";
    for (var i = 0; i < n; i++) {
        result += callback(i);
    }
    return result;
}
```

Notice how the implementation of buildString contains all the common parts of each loop, but uses a parameter in place of the parts that vary: The number of loop iterations becomes the variable n, and the construction of each string segment becomes a call to the callback function. We can now simplify each of the three examples to use buildString:

```
var alphabet = buildString(26, function(i) {
    return String.fromCharCode(aIndex + i);
});
alphabet; // "abcdefghijklmnopqrstuvwxyz"

var digits = buildString(10, function(i) { return i; });
digits; // "0123456789"

var random = buildString(8, function() {
    return String.fromCharCode(Math.floor(Math.random() * 26)
                               + aIndex);
});
random; // "ltvisfjr" (different result each time)
```

There are many benefits to creating higher-order abstractions. If there are tricky parts of the implementation, such as getting the loop boundary conditions right, they are localized to the implementation of the higher-order function. This allows you to fix any bugs in the logic just once, instead of having to hunt for every instance of the coding pattern spread throughout your program. If you find you need to optimize the efficiency of the operation, you again only have one place where you need to change anything. Finally, giving a clear name such as buildString to the abstraction makes it clearer to someone reading the code what the code does, without having to decode the details of the implementation.

Learning to reach for a higher-order function when you find yourself repeatedly writing the same patterns leads to more concise code, higher productivity, and improved readability. Keeping an eye out for common patterns and moving them into higher-order utility functions is an important habit to develop.

Things to Remember

✦ Higher-order functions are functions that take other functions as arguments or return functions as their result.

✦ Familiarize yourself with higher-order functions in existing libraries.

✦ Learn to detect common coding patterns that can be replaced by higher-order functions.

Item 20: Use call to Call Methods with a Custom Receiver

Ordinarily, the receiver of a function or method (i.e., the value bound to the special keyword this) is determined by the syntax of its caller. In particular, the method call syntax binds the object in which the method was looked up to this. However, it is sometimes necessary to call a function with a custom receiver, and the function may not already be a property of the desired receiver object. It's possible, of course, to add the method to the object as a new property:

```
obj.temporary = f;    // what if obj.temporary already existed?
var result = obj.temporary(arg1, arg2, arg3);
delete obj.temporary; // what if obj.temporary already existed?
```

But this approach is unpleasant and even dangerous. It is often undesirable, and even sometimes impossible, to modify obj. Specifically, whatever name you choose for the temporary property, you run the risk of colliding with an existing property of obj. Moreover, some objects can be frozen or sealed, preventing the addition of any new properties. And more generally, it's bad practice to go around arbitrarily adding properties to objects, particularly objects you didn't create (see Item 42).

Luckily, functions come with a built-in `call` method for providing a custom receiver. Invoking a function via its `call` method:

```
f.call(obj, arg1, arg2, arg3);
```

behaves similarly to calling it directly:

```
f(arg1, arg2, arg3);
```

except that the first argument provides an explicit receiver object.

The `call` method comes in handy for calling methods that may have been removed, modified, or overridden. Item 45 shows a useful example, where the `hasOwnProperty` method can be called on an arbitrary object, even if the object is a dictionary. In a dictionary object, looking up hasOwnProperty produces an entry from the dictionary rather than an inherited method:

```
dict.hasOwnProperty = 1;
dict.hasOwnProperty("foo"); // error: 1 is not a function
```

Using the `call` method of the `hasOwnProperty` method makes it possible to call the method on the dictionary even though the method is not stored anywhere in the object:

```
var hasOwnProperty = {}.hasOwnProperty;
dict.foo = 1;
delete dict.hasOwnProperty;
hasOwnProperty.call(dict, "foo");            // true
hasOwnProperty.call(dict, "hasOwnProperty"); // false
```

The `call` method can also be useful when defining higher-order functions. A common idiom for a higher-order function is to accept an optional argument to provide as the receiver for calling the function. For example, an object that represents a table of key-value bindings might provide a `forEach` method:

```
var table = {
    entries: [],
    addEntry: function(key, value) {
        this.entries.push({ key: key, value: value });
    },
    forEach: function(f, thisArg) {
        var entries = this.entries;
```

```
        for (var i = 0, n = entries.length; i < n; i++) {
            var entry = entries[i];
            f.call(thisArg, entry.key, entry.value, i);
        }
    }
};
```

This allows consumers of the object to use a method as the callback function f of table.forEach and provide a sensible receiver for the method. For example, we can conveniently copy the contents of one table into another:

```
table1.forEach(table2.addEntry, table2);
```

This code extracts the addEntry method from table2 (it could have even extracted the method from Table.prototype or table1), and the forEach method repeatedly calls addEntry with table2 as the receiver. Notice that even though addEntry only expects two arguments, forEach calls it with three: a key, value, and index. The extra index argument is harmless since addEntry simply ignores it.

Things to Remember

✦ Use the call method to call a function with a custom receiver.

✦ Use the call method for calling methods that may not exist on a given object.

✦ Use the call method for defining higher-order functions that allow clients to provide a receiver for the callback.

Item 21: Use apply to Call Functions with Different Numbers of Arguments

Imagine that someone provides us with a function that calculates the average of any number of values:

```
average(1, 2, 3);                       // 2
average(1);                             // 1
average(3, 1, 4, 1, 5, 9, 2, 6, 5);    // 4
average(2, 7, 1, 8, 2, 8, 1, 8);       // 4.625
```

The average function is an example of what's known as a *variadic* or *variable-arity* function (the *arity* of a function is the number of arguments it expects): It can take any number of arguments. By comparison, a fixed-arity version of average would probably take a single argument containing an array of values:

```
averageOfArray([1, 2, 3]);                    // 2
averageOfArray([1]);                          // 1
averageOfArray([3, 1, 4, 1, 5, 9, 2, 6, 5]); // 4
averageOfArray([2, 7, 1, 8, 2, 8, 1, 8]);    // 4.625
```

The variadic version is more concise and arguably more elegant. Variadic functions have convenient syntax, at least when the caller knows ahead of time exactly how many arguments to provide, as in the examples above. But imagine that we have an array of values:

```
var scores = getAllScores();
```

How can we use the average function to compute their average?

```
average(/* ? */);
```

Fortunately, functions come with a built-in apply method, which is similar to their call method, but designed just for this purpose. The apply method takes an array of arguments and calls the function as if each element of the array were an individual argument of the call. In addition to the array of arguments, the apply method takes a first argument that specifies the binding of this for the function being called. Since the average function does not refer to this, we can simply pass it null:

```
var scores = getAllScores();
average.apply(null, scores);
```

If scores turns out to have, say, three elements, this will behave the same as if we had written:

```
average(scores[0], scores[1], scores[2]);
```

The apply method can be used on variadic methods, too. For example, a buffer object might contain a variadic append method for adding entries to its internal state (see Item 22 to understand the implementation of append):

```
var buffer = {
    state: [],
    append: function() {
        for (var i = 0, n = arguments.length; i < n; i++) {
            this.state.push(arguments[i]);
        }
    }
};
```

The append method can be called with any number of arguments:

```
buffer.append("Hello, ");
buffer.append(firstName, " ", lastName, "!");
buffer.append(newline);
```

With the this argument of apply, we can also call append with a computed array:

```
buffer.append.apply(buffer, getInputStrings());
```

Notice the importance of the buffer argument: If we passed a different object, the append method would attempt to modify the state property of the wrong object.

Things to Remember

✦ Use the apply method to call variadic functions with a computed array of arguments.

✦ Use the first argument of apply to provide a receiver for variadic methods.

Item 22: Use arguments to Create Variadic Functions

Item 21 describes a variadic average function, which can process an arbitrary number of arguments and produce their average value. How can we implement a variadic function of our own? The fixed-arity version, averageOfArray, is easy enough to implement:

```
function averageOfArray(a) {
    for (var i = 0, sum = 0, n = a.length; i < n; i++) {
        sum += a[i];
    }
    return sum / n;
}
averageOfArray([2, 7, 1, 8, 2, 8, 1, 8]); // 4.625
```

The definition of averageOfArray defines a single *formal parameter*, the variable a in the parameter list. When consumers call averageOfArray, they provide a single argument (sometimes called an *actual argument* to distinguish it clearly from the formal parameter), the array of values.

The variadic version is almost identical, but it does not define any explicit formal parameters. Instead, it makes use of the fact that JavaScript provides every function with an implicit local variable called arguments. The arguments object provides an array-like interface to the actual arguments: It contains indexed properties for each actual argument and a length property indicating how many arguments were provided. This makes the variable-arity average function expressible by looping over each element of the `arguments` object:

```
function average() {
    for (var i = 0, sum = 0, n = arguments.length;
        i < n;
        i++) {
        sum += arguments[i];
    }
    return sum / n;
}
```

Variadic functions make for flexible interfaces; different clients can call them with different numbers of arguments. But by themselves, they also lose a bit of convenience: If consumers want to call them with a computed array of arguments, they have to use the `apply` method described in Item 21. A good rule of thumb is that whenever you provide a variable-arity function for convenience, you should also provide a fixed-arity version that takes an explicit array. This is usually easy to provide, because you can typically implement the variadic function as a small wrapper that delegates to the fixed-arity version:

```
function average() {
    return averageOfArray(arguments);
}
```

This way, consumers of your functions don't have to resort to the `apply` method, which can be less readable and often carries a performance cost.

Things to Remember

✦ Use the implicit `arguments` object to implement variable-arity functions.

✦ Consider providing additional fixed-arity versions of the variadic functions you provide so that your consumers don't need to use the `apply` method.

Item 23: Never Modify the `arguments` Object

The `arguments` object may look like an array, but sadly it does not always behave like one. Programmers familiar with Perl and UNIX shell scripting are accustomed to the technique of "shifting" elements off of the beginning of an array of arguments. And JavaScript's arrays do in fact contain a `shift` method, which removes the first element of an array and shifts all the subsequent elements over by one. But the arguments object itself is not an instance of the standard Array type, so we cannot directly call arguments.shift().

Thanks to the call method, you might expect to be able to extract the shift method from an array and call it on the arguments object. This might seem like a reasonable way to implement a function such as callMethod, which takes an object and a method name and attempts to call the object's method on all the remaining arguments:

```
function callMethod(obj, method) {
    var shift = [].shift;
    shift.call(arguments);
    shift.call(arguments);
    return obj[method].apply(obj, arguments);
}
```

But this function does not behave even remotely as expected:

```
var obj = {
    add: function(x, y) { return x + y; }
};
callMethod(obj, "add", 17, 25);
// error: cannot read property "apply" of undefined
```

The reason why this fails is that the arguments object is not a copy of the function's arguments. In particular, all named arguments are *aliases* to their corresponding indices in the arguments object. So obj continues to be an alias for arguments[0] and method for arguments[1], even after we remove elements from the arguments object via shift. This means that while we appear to be extracting obj["add"], we are actually extracting 17[25]! At this point, everything begins to go haywire: Thanks to the automatic coercion rules of JavaScript, this promotes 17 to a Number object, extracts its "25" property (which does not exist), produces undefined, and then unsuccessfully attempts to extract the "apply" property of undefined to call it as a method.

The moral of this story is that the relationship between the arguments object and the named parameters of a function is extremely brittle. Modifying arguments runs the risk of turning the named parameters of a function into gibberish. The situation is complicated even further by ES5's strict mode. Function parameters in strict mode do *not* alias their arguments object. We can demonstrate the difference by writing a function that updates an element of arguments:

```
function strict(x) {
    "use strict";
    arguments[0] = "modified";
```

```
    return x === arguments[0];
}
function nonstrict(x) {
    arguments[0] = "modified";
    return x === arguments[0];
}
strict("unmodified");     // false
nonstrict("unmodified"); // true
```

As a consequence, it is much safer never to modify the arguments object. This is easy enough to avoid by first copying its elements to a real array. A simple idiom for implementing the copy is:

```
var args = [].slice.call(arguments);
```

The slice method of arrays makes a copy of an array when called without additional arguments, and its result is a true instance of the standard Array type. The result is guaranteed not to alias anything, and has all the normal Array methods available to it directly.

We can fix the callMethod implementation by copying arguments, and since we only need the elements after obj and method, we can pass a starting index of 2 to slice:

```
function callMethod(obj, method) {
    var args = [].slice.call(arguments, 2);
    return obj[method].apply(obj, args);
}
```

At last, callMethod works as expected:

```
var obj = {
    add: function(x, y) { return x + y; }
};
callMethod(obj, "add", 17, 25); // 42
```

Things to Remember

✦ Never modify the arguments object.

✦ Copy the arguments object to a real array using [].slice.call(arguments) before modifying it.

Item 24: Use a Variable to Save a Reference to arguments

An *iterator* is an object providing sequential access to a collection of data. A typical API provides a next method that provides the next value in the sequence. Imagine we wish to write a convenience function that takes an arbitrary number of arguments and builds an iterator for those values:

```
var it = values(1, 4, 1, 4, 2, 1, 3, 5, 6);
it.next(); // 1
it.next(); // 4
it.next(); // 1
```

The values function must accept any number of arguments, so we construct our iterator object to iterate over the elements of the arguments object:

```
function values() {
    var i = 0, n = arguments.length;
    return {
        hasNext: function() {
            return i < n;
        },
        next: function() {
            if (i >= n) {
                throw new Error("end of iteration");
            }
            return arguments[i++]; // wrong arguments
        }
    };
}
```

But this code is broken, which becomes clear as soon as we attempt to use an iterator object:

```
var it = values(1, 4, 1, 4, 2, 1, 3, 5, 6);
it.next(); // undefined
it.next(); // undefined
it.next(); // undefined
```

The problem is due to the fact that a new arguments variable is implicitly bound in the body of each function. The arguments object we are interested in is the one associated with the values function, but the iterator's next method contains its own arguments variable. So when we return arguments[i++], we are accessing an argument of it.next instead of one of the arguments of values.

The solution is straightforward: Simply bind a new local variable in the scope of the arguments object we are interested in, and make sure that nested functions only refer to that explicitly named variable:

```
function values() {
    var i = 0, n = arguments.length, a = arguments;
    return {
```

```
        hasNext: function() {
            return i < n;
        },
        next: function() {
            if (i >= n) {
                throw new Error("end of iteration");
            }
            return a[i++];
        }
    };
}
var it = values(1, 4, 1, 4, 2, 1, 3, 5, 6);
it.next(); // 1
it.next(); // 4
it.next(); // 1
```

Things to Remember

✦ Be aware of the function nesting level when referring to `arguments`.

✦ Bind an explicitly scoped reference to `arguments` in order to refer to it from nested functions.

Item 25: Use bind to Extract Methods with a Fixed Receiver

With no distinction between a method and a property whose value is a function, it's easy to extract a method of an object and pass the extracted function directly as a callback to a higher-order function. But it's also easy to forget that an extracted function's receiver is not bound to the object it was taken from. Imagine a little string buffer object that stores strings in an array that can be concatenated later:

```
var buffer = {
    entries: [],
    add: function(s) {
        this.entries.push(s);
    },
    concat: function() {
        return this.entries.join("");
    }
};
```

It might seem possible to copy an array of strings into the buffer by extracting its add method and calling it repeatedly on each element of the source array using the ES5 forEach method:

```
var source = ["867", "-", "5309"];
source.forEach(buffer.add); // error: entries is undefined
```

But the receiver of `buffer.add` is not `buffer`. A function's receiver is determined by how it is called, and we are not calling it here. Instead, we pass it to `forEach`, whose implementation calls it somewhere that we can't see. As it turns out, the implementation of `forEach` uses the global object as the default receiver. Since the global object has no `entries` property, this code throws an error. Luckily, `forEach` also allows callers to provide an optional argument to use as the receiver of its callback, so we can fix this example easily enough:

```
var source = ["867", "-", "5309"];
source.forEach(buffer.add, buffer);
buffer.concat(); // "867-5309"
```

Not all higher-order functions offer their clients the courtesy of providing a receiver for their callbacks. What if `forEach` did not accept the extra receiver argument? A good solution is to create a local function that makes sure to call `buffer.add` with the appropriate method call syntax:

```
var source = ["867", "-", "5309"];
source.forEach(function(s) {
    buffer.add(s);
});
buffer.concat(); // "867-5309"
```

This version creates a wrapper function that explicitly calls `add` as a method of `buffer`. Notice how the wrapper function itself does not refer to `this` at all. No matter how the wrapper function is called—as a function, as a method of some other object, or via `call`—it always makes sure to push its argument on the destination array.

Creating a version of a function that binds its receiver to a specific object is so common that ES5 added library support for the pattern. Function objects come with a `bind` method that takes a receiver object and produces a wrapper function that calls the original function as a method of the receiver. Using `bind`, we can simplify our example:

```
var source = ["867", "-", "5309"];
source.forEach(buffer.add.bind(buffer));
buffer.concat(); // "867-5309"
```

Keep in mind that `buffer.add.bind(buffer)` creates a *new* function rather than modifying the `buffer.add` function. The new function behaves just like the old one, but with its receiver bound to `buffer`, while the old one remains unchanged. In other words:

```
buffer.add === buffer.add.bind(buffer); // false
```

This is a subtle but crucial point: It means that bind is safe to call even on a function that may be shared by other parts of a program. It is especially important for methods shared on a prototype object: The method will still work correctly when called on any of the prototype's descendants. (See Chapter 4 for more on objects and prototypes.)

Things to Remember

✦ Beware that extracting a method does not bind the method's receiver to its object.

✦ When passing an object's method to a higher-order function, use an anonymous function to call the method on the appropriate receiver.

✦ Use bind as a shorthand for creating a function bound to the appropriate receiver.

Item 26: Use bind to Curry Functions

The bind method of functions is useful for more than just binding methods to receivers. Imagine a simple function for constructing URL strings from components:

```
function simpleURL(protocol, domain, path) {
    return protocol + "://" + domain + "/" + path;
}
```

Frequently, a program may need to construct absolute URLs from site-specific path strings. A natural way to do this is with the ES5 map method on arrays:

```
var urls = paths.map(function(path) {
    return simpleURL("http", siteDomain, path);
});
```

Notice how the anonymous function uses the same protocol string and the same site domain string on each iteration of map; the first two arguments to simpleURL are fixed for each iteration, and only the third argument is needed. We can use the bind method on simpleURL to construct this function automatically:

```
var urls = paths.map(simpleURL.bind(null, "http", siteDomain));
```

The call to simpleURL.bind produces a new function that delegates to simpleURL. As always, the first argument to bind provides the receiver value. (Since simpleURL does not refer to this, we can use any value; `null` and `undefined` are customary.) The arguments passed to `simpleURL` are constructed by concatenating the remaining arguments of `simpleURL.bind` to any arguments provided to the new function. In other words, when the result of `simpleURL.bind` is called with a single argument `path`, the function delegates to `simpleURL("http", siteDomain, path)`.

The technique of binding a function to a subset of its arguments is known as *currying,* named after the logician Haskell Curry, who popularized the technique in mathematics. Currying can be a succinct way to implement function delegation with less boilerplate than explicit wrapper functions.

Things to Remember

✦ Use `bind` to curry a function, that is, to create a delegating function with a fixed subset of the required arguments.

✦ Pass `null` or `undefined` as the receiver argument to curry a function that ignores its receiver.

Item 27: Prefer Closures to Strings for Encapsulating Code

Functions are a convenient way to store code as a data structure that can be executed later. This enables expressive higher-order abstractions such as `map` and `forEach`, and it is at the heart of JavaScript's asynchronous approach to I/O (see Chapter 7). At the same time, it's also possible to represent code as a string to pass to `eval`. Programmers are then confronted with a decision to make: Should code be represented as a function or as a string?

When in doubt, use a function. Strings are a much less flexible representation of code for one very important reason: They are not closures.

Consider a simple function for repeating a user-provided action multiple times:

```
function repeat(n, action) {
    for (var i = 0; i < n; i++) {
        eval(action);
    }
}
```

At global scope, using this function will work reasonably well, because any variable references that occur within the string will be interpreted by `eval` as global variables. For example, a script that benchmarks the speed of a function might just use global `start` and end variables to store the timings:

```
var start = [], end = [], timings = [];
repeat(1000,
        "start.push(Date.now()); f(); end.push(Date.now())");
for (var i = 0, n = start.length; i < n; i++) {
    timings[i] = end[i] - start[i];
}
```

But this script is brittle. If we simply move the code into a function, then `start` and end are no longer global variables:

```
function benchmark() {
    var start = [], end = [], timings = [];
    repeat(1000,
            "start.push(Date.now()); f(); end.push(Date.now())");
    for (var i = 0, n = start.length; i < n; i++) {
        timings[i] = end[i] - start[i];
    }
    return timings;
}
```

This function causes `repeat` to evaluate references to the global variables `start` and end. In the best case, one of the globals will be missing, and calling benchmark will throw a `ReferenceError`. If we're really unlucky, the code will actually call push on some global objects that happen to be bound to `start` and end, and the program will behave unpredictably.

A more robust API accepts a function instead of a string:

```
function repeat(n, action) {
    for (var i = 0; i < n; i++) {
        action();
    }
}
```

This way, the benchmark script can safely refer to local variables within a closure that it passes as the repeated callback:

```
function benchmark() {
    var start = [], end = [], timings = [];
    repeat(1000, function() {
        start.push(Date.now());
        f();
```

```
        end.push(Date.now());
    });
    for (var i = 0, n = start.length; i < n; i++) {
        timings[i] = end[i] - start[i];
    }
    return timings;
}
```

Another problem with eval is that high-performance engines typically have a harder time optimizing code inside a string, since the source code may not be available to the compiler early enough to optimize in time. A function expression can be compiled at the same time as the code it appears within, making it much more amenable to standard compilation.

Things to Remember

✦ Never include local references in strings when sending them to APIs that execute them with eval.

✦ Prefer APIs that accept functions to call rather than strings to eval.

Item 28: Avoid Relying on the toString Method of Functions

JavaScript functions come with a remarkable feature—the ability to reproduce their source code as a string:

```
(function(x) {
    return x + 1;
}).toString(); // "function (x) {\n      return x + 1;\n}"
```

Reflecting on the source code of a function is powerful, and clever hackers occasionally find ingenious ways to put it to use. But there are serious limitations to the toString method of functions.

First of all, the ECMAScript standard does not impose any requirements on the string that results from a function's toString method. This means that different JavaScript engines will produce different strings, and may not even produce strings that bear any resemblance to the function.

In practice, JavaScript engines *do* attempt to provide a faithful representation of the source code of a function, as long as the function was implemented in pure JavaScript. An example of where this fails is with functions produced by built-in libraries of the host environment:

```
(function(x) {
    return x + 1;
}).bind(16).toString(); // "function (x) {\n    [native code]\n}"
```

Since in many host environments, the bind function is implemented in another programming language (typically C++), it produces a compiled function that has no JavaScript source code for the environment to reveal.

Because browser engines are allowed by the standard to vary in their output from toString, it is all too easy to write a program that works correctly in one JavaScript system but fails in another. JavaScript implementations will even make small changes (e.g., the whitespace formatting) that could break a program that is too sensitive to the exact details of function source strings.

Finally, the source code produced by toString does not provide a representation of closures that preserves the values associated with their inner variable references. For example:

```
(function(x) {
    return function(y) {
        return x + y;
    }
})(42).toString(); // "function (y) {\n    return x + y;\n}"
```

Notice how the resultant string still contains a variable reference to x, even though the function is actually a closure that binds x to 42.

These limitations make it difficult to depend on extracting function source in a manner that is both useful and reliable, and should generally be avoided. Very sophisticated uses of function source extraction should employ carefully crafted JavaScript parsers and processing libraries. But when in doubt, it's safest to treat a JavaScript function as an abstraction that should not be broken.

Things to Remember

+ JavaScript engines are not required to produce accurate reflections of function source code via toString.

+ Never rely on precise details of function source, since different engines may produce different results from toString.

+ The results of toString do not expose the values of local variables stored in a closure.

+ In general, avoid using toString on functions.

Item 29: Avoid Nonstandard Stack Inspection Properties

Many JavaScript environments have historically provided some capabilities to inspect the *call stack*: the chain of active functions that are currently executing (see Item 64 for more about the call stack). In some older host environments, every arguments object came with two additional properties: arguments.callee, which refers to the function that was called with arguments, and arguments.caller, which refers to the function that called it. The former is still supported in many environments, but it does not serve much of a purpose, short of allowing anonymous functions to refer to themselves recursively:

```
var factorial = (function(n) {
    return (n <= 1) ? 1 : (n * arguments.callee(n - 1));
});
```

But this is not particularly useful, since it's more straightforward for a function just to refer to itself by name:

```
function factorial(n) {
    return (n <= 1) ? 1 : (n * factorial(n - 1));
}
```

The arguments.caller property is more powerful: It refers to the function that made the call with the given arguments object. This feature has since been removed from most environments out of security concerns, so it's not reliable. Many JavaScript environments also provide a similar property of function objects—the nonstandard but widespread caller property, which refers to the function's most recent caller:

```
function revealCaller() {
    return revealCaller.caller;
}

function start() {
    return revealCaller();
}

start() === start; // true
```

It is tempting to try to use this property to extract a *stack trace:* a data structure providing a snapshot of the current call stack. Building a stack trace seems deceptively simple:

```
function getCallStack() {
    var stack = [];
```

```
    for (var f = getCallStack.caller; f; f = f.caller) {
        stack.push(f);
    }
    return stack;
}
```

For simple call stacks, getCallStack appears to work fine:

```
function f1() {
    return getCallStack();
}

function f2() {
    return f1();
}

var trace = f2();
trace; // [f1, f2]
```

But getCallStack is easily broken: If a function shows up more than once in the call stack, the stack inspection logic gets stuck in a loop!

```
function f(n) {
    return n === 0 ? getCallStack() : f(n - 1);
}

var trace = f(1); // infinite loop
```

What went wrong? Since the function f calls itself recursively, its caller property is automatically updated to refer back to f. So the loop in getCallStack gets stuck perpetually looking at f. Even if we tried to detect such cycles, there's no information about what function called f before it called itself—the information about the rest of the call stack is lost.

Each of these stack inspection facilities is nonstandard and limited in portability or applicability. Moreover, they are all explicitly disallowed in ES5 strict functions; attempted accesses to the caller or callee properties of strict functions or arguments objects throw an error:

```
function f() {
    "use strict";
    return f.caller;
}

f(); // error: caller may not be accessed on strict functions
```

The best policy is to avoid stack inspection altogether. If your reason for inspecting the stack is solely for debugging, it's much more reliable to use an interactive debugger.

Things to Remember

+ Avoid the nonstandard `arguments.caller` and `arguments.callee`, because they are not reliably portable.

+ Avoid the nonstandard `caller` property of functions, because it does not reliably contain complete information about the stack.

Objects and Prototypes

Objects are JavaScript's fundamental data structure. Intuitively, an object represents a table relating strings to values. But when you dig deeper, there is a fair amount of machinery that goes into objects.

Like many object-oriented languages, JavaScript provides support for *implementation inheritance:* the reuse of code or data through a dynamic delegation mechanism. But unlike many conventional languages, JavaScript's inheritance mechanism is based on prototypes rather than classes. For many programmers, JavaScript is the first object-oriented language they encounter without classes.

In many languages, every object is an instance of an associated class, which provides code shared between all its instances. JavaScript, by contrast, has no built-in notion of classes. Instead, objects inherit from other objects. Every object is associated with some other object, known as its *prototype.* Working with prototypes can be different from classes, although many concepts from traditional object-oriented languages still carry over.

Item 30: Understand the Difference between prototype, getPrototypeOf, and __proto__

Prototypes involve three separate but related accessors, all of which are named with some variation on the word *prototype.* This unfortunate overlap naturally leads to quite a bit of confusion. Let's get straight to the point.

- `C.prototype` is used to establish the prototype of objects created by new `C()`.

- `Object.getPrototypeOf(obj)` is the standard ES5 mechanism for retrieving obj's prototype object.

- obj.__proto__ is a nonstandard mechanism for retrieving obj's prototype object.

To understand each of these, consider a typical definition of a JavaScript datatype. The User constructor expects to be called with the new operator and takes a name and the hash of a password string and stores them on its created object.

```
function User(name, passwordHash) {
    this.name = name;
    this.passwordHash = passwordHash;
}

User.prototype.toString = function() {
    return "[User " + this.name + "]";
};

User.prototype.checkPassword = function(password) {
    return hash(password) === this.passwordHash;
};

var u = new User("sfalken",
                 "0ef33ae791068ec64b502d6cb0191387");
```

The User function comes with a default prototype property, containing an object that starts out more or less empty. In this example, we add two methods to the User.prototype object: toString and checkPassword. When we create an instance of User with the new operator, the resultant object u gets the object stored at User.prototype automatically assigned as its prototype object. Figure 4.1 shows a diagram of these objects.

Notice the arrow linking the instance object u to the prototype object User.prototype. This link describes the inheritance relationship. Property lookups start by searching the object's *own properties;* for example, u.name and u.passwordHash return the current values of immediate properties of u. Properties not found directly on u are looked up in u's prototype. Accessing u.checkPassword, for example, retrieves a method stored in User.prototype.

This leads us to the next item in our list. Whereas the prototype property of a constructor function is used to set up the prototype relationship of new instances, the ES5 function Object.getPrototypeOf() can be used to retrieve the prototype of an existing object. So, for example, after we create the object u in the example above, we can test:

```
Object.getPrototypeOf(u) === User.prototype; // true
```

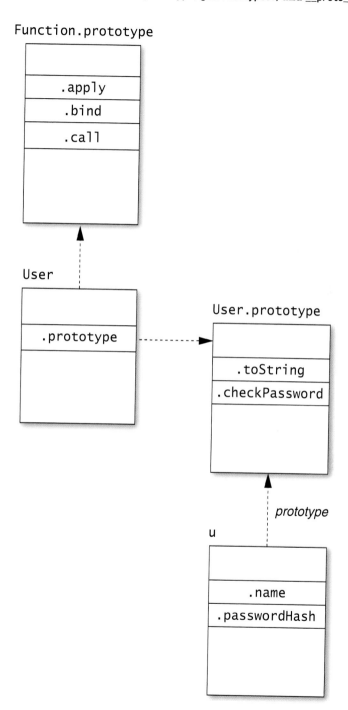

Figure 4.1 Prototype relationships for the User constructor and instance

Some environments produce a nonstandard mechanism for retrieving the prototype of an object via a special __proto__ property. This can be useful as a stopgap for environments that do not support ES5's Object.getPrototypeOf. In such environments, we can similarly test:

u.__proto__ === User.prototype; // *true*

A final note about prototype relationships: JavaScript programmers will often describe User as a *class*, even though it consists of little more than a function. Classes in JavaScript are essentially the combination of a constructor function (User) and a prototype object used to share methods between instances of the class (User.prototype).

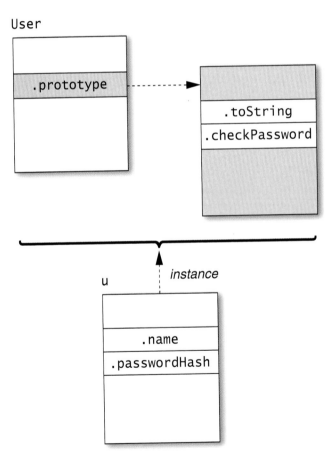

Figure 4.2 Conceptual view of the User "class"

Figure 4.2 provides a good way to think about the User class conceptually. The User function provides a public constructor for the class, and User.prototype is an internal implementation of the methods shared between instances. Ordinary uses of User and u have no need to access the prototype object directly.

Things to Remember

✦ `C.prototype` determines the prototype of objects created by `new C()`.

✦ `Object.getPrototypeOf(obj)` is the standard ES5 function for retrieving the prototype of an object.

✦ `obj.__proto__` is a nonstandard mechanism for retrieving the prototype of an object.

✦ A class is a design pattern consisting of a constructor function and an associated prototype.

Item 31: Prefer `Object.getPrototypeOf` to `__proto__`

ES5 introduced `Object.getPrototypeOf` as the standard API for retrieving an object's prototype, but only after a number of JavaScript engines had long provided the special `__proto__` property for the same purpose. Not all JavaScript environments support this extension, however, and those that do are not entirely compatible. Environments differ, for example, on the treatment of objects with a null prototype. In some environments, `__proto__` is inherited from `Object.prototype`, so an object with a null prototype has no special `__proto__` property:

```
var empty = Object.create(null); // object with no prototype
"__proto__" in empty; // false (in some environments)
```

In others, `__proto__` is always handled specially, regardless of an object's state:

```
var empty = Object.create(null); // object with no prototype
"__proto__" in empty; // true (in some environments)
```

Wherever `Object.getPrototypeOf` is available, it is the more standard and portable approach to extracting prototypes. Moreover, the `__proto__` property leads to a number of bugs due to its pollution of all objects (see Item 45). JavaScript engines that currently support the extension may choose in the future to allow programs to disable it in order to avoid these bugs. Preferring `Object.getPrototypeOf` ensures that code will continue to work even if `__proto__` is disabled.

For JavaScript environments that do not provide the ES5 API, it is easy to implement in terms of __proto__:

```
if (typeof Object.getPrototypeOf === "undefined") {
    Object.getPrototypeOf = function(obj) {
        var t = typeof obj;
        if (!obj || (t !== "object" && t !== "function")) {
            throw new TypeError("not an object");
        }
        return obj.__proto__;
    };
}
```

This implementation is safe to include in ES5 environments, because it avoids installing the function if Object.getPrototypeOf already exists.

Things to Remember

✦ Prefer the standards-compliant Object.getPrototypeOf to the non-standard __proto__ property.

✦ Implement Object.getPrototypeOf in non-ES5 environments that support __proto__.

Item 32: Never Modify __proto__

The special __proto__ property provides an additional power that Object.getPrototypeOf does not: the ability to *modify* an object's prototype link. While this power may seem innocuous (after all, it's just another property, right?), it actually has serious implications and should be avoided. The most obvious reason to avoid modifying __proto__ is portability: Since not all platforms support the ability to change an object's prototype you simply can't write portable code that does it.

Another reason to avoid modifying __proto__ is performance. All modern JavaScript engines heavily optimize the act of getting and setting object properties, since these are some of the most common operations that JavaScript programs perform. These optimizations are built on the engine's knowledge of the structure of an object. When you change the object's internal structure, say, by adding or removing properties to the object or an object in its prototype chain, some of these optimizations are invalidated. Modifying __proto__ actually changes the inheritance structure itself, which is the most destructive change possible. This can invalidate many more optimizations than modifications to ordinary properties.

But the biggest reason to avoid modifying __proto__ is for maintaining predictable behavior. An object's prototype chain defines its behavior by determining its set of properties and property values. Modifying an object's prototype link is like giving it a brain transplant: It swaps the object's entire inheritance hierarchy. It may be possible to imagine exceptional situations where such an operation could be helpful, but as a matter of basic sanity, an inheritance hierarchy should remain stable.

For creating new objects with a custom prototype link, you can use ES5's Object.create. For environments that do not implement ES5, Item 33 provides a portable implementation of Object.create that does not rely on __proto__.

Things to Remember

✦ Never modify an object's __proto__ property.

✦ Use Object.create to provide a custom prototype for new objects.

Item 33: Make Your Constructors new-Agnostic

When you create a constructor such as the User function in Item 30, you rely on callers to remember to call it with the new operator. Notice how the function assumes that the receiver is a brand-new object:

```
function User(name, passwordHash) {
    this.name = name;
    this.passwordHash = passwordHash;
}
```

If a caller forgets the new keyword, then the function's receiver becomes the global object:

```
var u = User("baravelli", "d8b74df393528d51cd19980ae0aa028e");
u;                      // undefined
this.name;              // "baravelli"
this.passwordHash;      // "d8b74df393528d51cd19980ae0aa028e"
```

Not only does the function uselessly return undefined, it also disastrously creates (or modifies, if they happen to exist already) the global variables name and passwordHash.

If the User function is defined as ES5 strict code, then the receiver defaults to undefined:

```
function User(name, passwordHash) {
    "use strict";
    this.name = name;
```

```
    this.passwordHash = passwordHash;
}

var u = User("baravelli", "d8b74df393528d51cd19980ae0aa028e");
// error: this is undefined
```

In this case, the faulty call leads to an immediate error: The first line of User attempts to assign to this.name, which throws a TypeError. So, at least with a strict constructor function, the caller can quickly discover the bug and fix it.

Still, in either case, the User function is fragile. When used with new it works as expected, but when used as a normal function it fails. A more robust approach is to provide a function that works as a constructor no matter how it's called. An easy way to implement this is to check that the receiver value is a proper instance of User:

```
function User(name, passwordHash) {
    if (!(this instanceof User)) {
        return new User(name, passwordHash);
    }
    this.name = name;
    this.passwordHash = passwordHash;
}
```

This way, the result of calling User is an object that inherits from User.prototype, regardless of whether it's called as a function or as a constructor:

```
var x = User("baravelli", "d8b74df393528d51cd19980ae0aa028e");
var y = new User("baravelli",
                 "d8b74df393528d51cd19980ae0aa028e");
x instanceof User; // true
y instanceof User; // true
```

One downside to this pattern is that it requires an extra function call, so it is a bit more expensive. It's also hard to use for variadic functions (see Items 21 and 22), since there is no straightforward analog to the apply method for calling variadic functions as constructors. A somewhat more exotic approach makes use of ES5's Object.create:

```
function User(name, passwordHash) {
    var self = this instanceof User
             ? this
             : Object.create(User.prototype);
    self.name = name;
    self.passwordHash = passwordHash;
```

```
    return self;
}
```

`Object.create` takes a prototype object and returns a new object that inherits from it. So when this version of `User` is called as a function, the result is a new object inheriting from `User.prototype`, with the name and `passwordHash` properties initialized.

While `Object.create` is only available in ES5, it can be approximated in older environments by creating a local constructor and instantiating it with `new`:

```
if (typeof Object.create === "undefined") {
    Object.create = function(prototype) {
        function C() { }
        C.prototype = prototype;
        return new C();
    };
}
```

(Note that this only implements the single-argument version of `Object.create`. The real version also accepts an optional second argument that describes a set of property descriptors to define on the new object.)

What happens if someone calls this new version of `User` with `new`? Thanks to the *constructor override* pattern, it behaves just like it does with a function call. This works because JavaScript allows the result of a `new` expression to be overridden by an explicit `return` from a constructor function. When `User` returns `self`, the result of the `new` expression becomes `self`, which may be a different object from the one bound to `this`.

Protecting a constructor against misuse may not always be worth the trouble, especially when you are only using a constructor locally. Still, it's important to understand how badly things can go wrong if a constructor is called in the wrong way. At the very least, it's important to document when a constructor function expects to be called with `new`, especially when sharing it across a large codebase or from a shared library.

Things to Remember

+ Make a constructor agnostic to its caller's syntax by reinvoking itself with `new` or with `Object.create`.

+ Document clearly when a function expects to be called with `new`.

Item 34: Store Methods on Prototypes

It's perfectly possible to program in JavaScript without prototypes. We could implement the User class from Item 30 without defining anything special in its prototype:

```
function User(name, passwordHash) {
    this.name = name;
    this.passwordHash = passwordHash;
    this.toString = function() {
        return "[User " + this.name + "]";
    };
    this.checkPassword = function(password) {
        return hash(password) === this.passwordHash;
    };
}
```

For most purposes, this class behaves pretty much the same as its original implementation. But when we construct several instances of User, an important difference emerges:

```
var u1 = new User(/* ... */);
var u2 = new User(/* ... */);
var u3 = new User(/* ... */);
```

Figure 4.3 shows what these three objects and their prototype object look like. Instead of sharing the toString and checkPassword methods via the prototype, each instance contains a copy of both methods, for a total of six function objects.

By contrast, Figure 4.4 shows what these three objects and their prototype object look like using the original definition. The toString and checkPassword methods are created once and shared between all instances through their prototype.

Storing methods on a prototype makes them available to all instances without requiring multiple copies of the functions that implement them or extra properties on each instance object. You might expect that storing methods on instance objects could optimize the speed of method lookups such as u3.toString(), since it doesn't have to search the prototype chain to find the implementation of toString. However, modern JavaScript engines heavily optimize prototype lookups, so copying methods onto instance objects is not necessarily guaranteed to provide noticeable speed improvements. And instance methods are almost certain to use more memory than prototype methods.

User.prototype

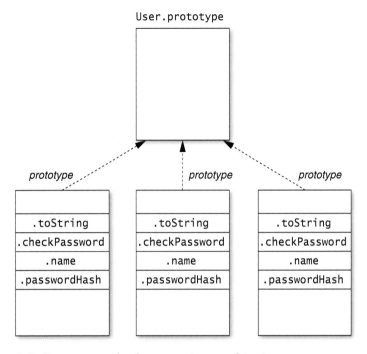

Figure 4.3 Storing methods on instance objects

User.prototype

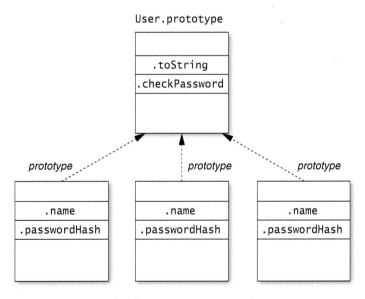

Figure 4.4 Storing methods on a prototype object

Things to Remember

✦ Storing methods on instance objects creates multiple copies of the functions, one per instance object.

✦ Prefer storing methods on prototypes over storing them on instance objects.

Item 35: Use Closures to Store Private Data

JavaScript's object system does not particularly encourage or enforce information hiding. The name of every property is a string, and any piece of a program can get access to any of the properties of an object simply by asking for it by name. Features such as for...in loops and ES5's `Object.keys()` and `Object.getOwnPropertyNames()` functions even make it easy to learn all the property names of an object.

Often, JavaScript programmers resort to coding conventions rather than any absolute enforcement mechanism for private properties. For example, some programmers use naming conventions such as prefixing or suffixing private property names with an underscore character (_). This does nothing to enforce information hiding, but it suggests to well-behaved users of an object that they should not inspect or modify the property so that the object can remain free to change its implementation.

Nevertheless, some programs actually call for a higher degree of hiding. For example, a security-sensitive platform or application framework may wish to send an object to an untrusted application without risk of the application tampering with the internals of the object. Another situation where enforcement of information hiding can be useful is in heavily used libraries, where subtle bugs can crop up when careless users accidentally depend on or interfere with implementation details.

For these situations, JavaScript does provide one very reliable mechanism for information hiding: the closure.

Closures are an austere data structure. They store data in their enclosed variables without providing direct access to those variables. The only way to gain access to the internals of a closure is for the function to provide access to it explicitly. In other words, objects and closures have opposite policies: The properties of an object are automatically exposed, whereas the variables in a closure are automatically hidden.

We can take advantage of this to store truly private data in an object. Instead of storing the data as properties of the object, we store it as variables in the constructor, and turn the methods of the object into closures that refer to those variables. Let's revisit the User class from Item 30 once more:

```
function User(name, passwordHash) {
    this.toString = function() {
        return "[User " + name + "]";
    };
    this.checkPassword = function(password) {
        return hash(password) === passwordHash;
    };
}
```

Notice how, unlike in other implementations, the toString and checkPassword methods refer to name and passwordHash as variables, rather than as properties of this. An instance of User now contains no instance properties at all, so outside code has no direct access to the name and password hash of an instance of User.

A downside to this pattern is that, in order for the variables of the constructor to be in scope of the methods that use them, the methods must be placed on the instance object. Just as Item 34 discussed, this can lead to a proliferation of copies of methods. Nevertheless, in situations where guaranteed information hiding is critical, it may be worth the additional cost.

Things to Remember

+ Closure variables are private, accessible only to local references.

+ Use local variables as private data to enforce information hiding within methods.

Item 36: Store Instance State Only on Instance Objects

Understanding the one-to-many relationship between a prototype object and its instances is crucial to implementing objects that behave correctly. One of the ways this can go wrong is by accidentally storing per-instance data on a prototype. For example, a class implementing a tree data structure might contain an array of children for each node. Putting the array of children on the prototype object leads to a completely broken implementation:

```
function Tree(x) {
    this.value = x;
}
```

```
Tree.prototype = {
    children: [],              // should be instance state!
    addChild: function(x) {
        this.children.push(x);
    }
};
```

Consider what happens when we try to construct a tree with this class:

```
var left = new Tree(2);
left.addChild(1);
left.addChild(3);

var right = new Tree(6);
right.addChild(5);
right.addChild(7);

var top = new Tree(4);
top.addChild(left);
top.addChild(right);

top.children; // [1, 3, 5, 7, left, right]
```

Each time we call addChild, we append a value to Tree.prototype
.children, which contains the nodes in the order of *any* calls to
addChild anywhere! This leaves the Tree objects in the incoherent
state shown in Figure 4.5.

The correct way to implement the Tree class is to create a separate
children array for each instance object:

```
function Tree(x) {
    this.value = x;
    this.children = []; // instance state
}
Tree.prototype = {
    addChild: function(x) {
        this.children.push(x);
    }
};
```

Running the same example code above, we get the expected state,
shown in Figure 4.6.

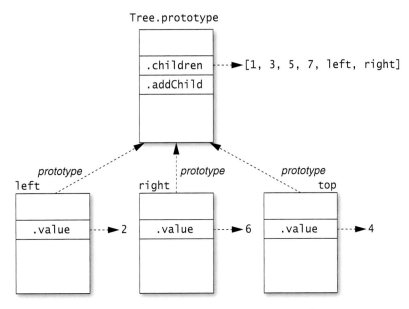

Figure 4.5 Storing instance state on a prototype object

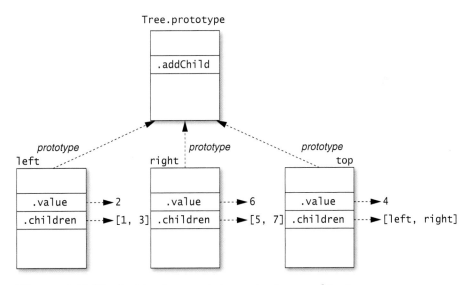

Figure 4.6 Storing instance state on instance objects

The moral of this story is that stateful data can be problematic when shared. Methods are generally safe to share between multiple instances of a class because they are typically stateless, other than referring to instance state via references to this. (Since the method call syntax ensures that this is bound to the instance object even for a method inherited from a prototype, shared methods can still access instance state.) In general, any immutable data is safe to share on a prototype, and stateful data can in principle be stored on a prototype, too, so long as it's truly intended to be shared. But methods are by far the most common data found on prototype objects. Per-instance state, meanwhile, must be stored on instance objects.

Things to Remember

✦ Mutable data can be problematic when shared, and prototypes are shared between all their instances.

✦ Store mutable per-instance state on instance objects.

Item 37: Recognize the Implicit Binding of this

The CSV (comma-separated values) file format is a simple text representation for tabular data:

```
Bösendorfer,1828,Vienna,Austria
Fazioli,1981,Sacile,Italy
Steinway,1853,New York,USA
```

We can write a simple, customizable class for reading CSV data. (For simplicity, we'll leave off the ability to parse quoted entries such as "hello, world".) Despite its name, CSV comes in different varieties allowing different characters for separators. So our constructor takes an optional array of separator characters and constructs a custom regular expression to use for splitting each line into entries:

```
function CSVReader(separators) {
    this.separators = separators || [","];
    this.regexp =
        new RegExp(this.separators.map(function(sep) {
            return "\\" + sep[0];
        }).join("|"));
}
```

A simple implementation of a read method can proceed in two steps: First, split the input string into an array of individual lines; second, split each line of the array into individual cells. The result should then be a two-dimensional array of strings. This is a perfect job for the map method:

```
CSVReader.prototype.read = function(str) {
    var lines = str.trim().split(/\n/);
    return lines.map(function(line) {
        return line.split(this.regexp); // wrong this!
    });
};
```

```
var reader = new CSVReader();
reader.read("a,b,c\nd,e,f\n"); // [["a,b,c"], ["d,e,f"]]
```

This seemingly simple code has a major but subtle bug: The callback passed to lines.map refers to this, expecting to extract the regexp property of the CSVReader object. But map binds its callback's receiver to the lines array, which has no such property. The result: this.regexp produces undefined, and the call to line.split goes haywire.

This bug is the result of the fact that this is bound in a different way from variables. As Items 18 and 25 explain, every function has an implicit binding of this, whose value is determined when the function is called. With a lexically scoped variable, you can always tell where it receives its binding by looking for an explicitly named *binding occurrence* of the name: for example, in a var declaration list or as a function parameter. By contrast, this is implicitly bound by the nearest enclosing function. So the binding of this in CSVReader.prototype.read is different from the binding of this in the callback function passed to lines.map.

Luckily, similar to the forEach example in Item 25, we can take advantage of the fact that the map method of arrays takes an optional second argument to use as a this-binding for the callback. So in this case, the easiest fix is to forward the outer binding of this to the callback by way of the second map argument:

```
CSVReader.prototype.read = function(str) {
    var lines = str.trim().split(/\n/);
    return lines.map(function(line) {
        return line.split(this.regexp);
    }, this); // forward outer this-binding to callback
};
```

```
var reader = new CSVReader();
reader.read("a,b,c\nd,e,f\n");
// [["a","b","c"], ["d","e","f"]]
```

Now, not all callback-based APIs are so considerate. What if `map` did not accept this additional argument? We would need another way to retain access to the outer function's this-binding so that the callback could still refer to it. The solution is straightforward enough: Just use a lexically scoped variable to save an additional reference to the outer binding of this:

```
CSVReader.prototype.read = function(str) {
    var lines = str.trim().split(/\n/);
    var self = this; // save a reference to outer this-binding
    return lines.map(function(line) {
        return line.split(self.regexp); // use outer this
    });
};
```

```
var reader = new CSVReader();
reader.read("a,b,c\nd,e,f\n");
// [["a","b","c"], ["d","e","f"]]
```

Programmers commonly use the variable name `self` for this pattern, signaling that the only purpose for the variable is as an extra alias to the current scope's this-binding. (Other popular variable names for this pattern are `me` and `that`.) The particular choice of name is not of great importance, but using a common name makes it easier for other programmers to recognize the pattern quickly.

Yet another valid approach in ES5 is to use the callback function's bind method, similar to the approach described in Item 25:

```
CSVReader.prototype.read = function(str) {
    var lines = str.trim().split(/\n/);
    return lines.map(function(line) {
        return line.split(this.regexp);
    }.bind(this)); // bind to outer this-binding
};
```

```
var reader = new CSVReader();
reader.read("a,b,c\nd,e,f\n");
// [["a","b","c"], ["d","e","f"]]
```

Things to Remember

✦ The scope of this is always determined by its nearest enclosing function.

✦ Use a local variable, usually called self, me, or that, to make a this-binding available to inner functions.

Item 38: Call Superclass Constructors from Subclass Constructors

A *scene graph* is a collection of objects describing a scene in a visual program such as a game or graphical simulation. A simple scene contains a collection of all of the objects in the scene, known as *actors,* a table of preloaded image data for the actors, and a reference to the underlying graphics display, often known as the *context:*

```
function Scene(context, width, height, images) {
    this.context = context;
    this.width = width;
    this.height = height;
    this.images = images;
    this.actors = [];
}

Scene.prototype.register = function(actor) {
    this.actors.push(actor);
};

Scene.prototype.unregister = function(actor) {
    var i = this.actors.indexOf(actor);
    if (i >= 0) {
        this.actors.splice(i, 1);
    }
};

Scene.prototype.draw = function() {
    this.context.clearRect(0, 0, this.width, this.height);
    for (var a = this.actors, i = 0, n = a.length;
         i < n;
         i++) {
        a[i].draw();
    }
};
```

All actors in a scene inherit from a base Actor class, which abstracts out common methods. Every actor stores a reference to its scene along with coordinate positions and then adds itself to the scene's actor registry:

```
function Actor(scene, x, y) {
    this.scene = scene;
    this.x = x;
    this.y = y;
    scene.register(this);
}
```

To enable changing an actor's position in the scene, we provide a moveTo method, which changes its coordinates and then redraws the scene:

```
Actor.prototype.moveTo = function(x, y) {
    this.x = x;
    this.y = y;
    this.scene.draw();
};
```

When an actor leaves the scene, we remove it from the scene graph's registry and redraw the scene:

```
Actor.prototype.exit = function() {
    this.scene.unregister(this);
    this.scene.draw();
};
```

To draw an actor, we look up its image in the scene graph image table. We'll assume that every actor has a type field that can be used to look up its image in the image table. Once we have this image data, we can draw it onto the graphics context, using the underlying graphics library. (This example uses the HTML Canvas API, which provides a drawImage method for drawing an Image object onto a <canvas> element in a web page.)

```
Actor.prototype.draw = function() {
    var image = this.scene.images[this.type];
    this.scene.context.drawImage(image, this.x, this.y);
};
```

Similarly, we can determine an actor's size from its image data:

```
Actor.prototype.width = function() {
    return this.scene.images[this.type].width;
};

Actor.prototype.height = function() {
    return this.scene.images[this.type].height;
};
```

We implement specific types of actors as subclasses of Actor. For example, a spaceship in an arcade game would have a SpaceShip class that extends Actor. Like all classes, SpaceShip is defined as a constructor function. But in order to ensure that instances of SpaceShip are properly initialized as actors, the constructor must explicitly call the Actor constructor. We do this by invoking Actor with the receiver bound to the new object:

```
function SpaceShip(scene, x, y) {
    Actor.call(this, scene, x, y);
    this.points = 0;
}
```

Calling the Actor constructor first ensures that all the instance properties created by Actor are added to the new object. After that, SpaceShip can define its own instance properties such as the ship's current points count.

In order for SpaceShip to be a proper subclass of Actor, its prototype must inherit from Actor.prototype. The best way to do the extension is with ES5's Object.create:

```
SpaceShip.prototype = Object.create(Actor.prototype);
```

(Item 33 describes an implementation of Object.create for environments that do not support ES5.) If we had tried to create SpaceShip's prototype object with the Actor constructor, there would be several problems. The first problem is that we don't have any reasonable arguments to pass to Actor:

```
SpaceShip.prototype = new Actor();
```

When we initialize the SpaceShip prototype, we haven't yet created any scenes to pass as the first argument. And the SpaceShip prototype doesn't have a useful x or y coordinate. These properties should be instance properties of individual SpaceShip objects, not properties of SpaceShip.prototype. More problematically, the Actor constructor adds the object to the scene's registry, which we definitely do not want to do with the SpaceShip prototype. This is a common phenomenon with subclasses: The superclass constructor should only be invoked from the subclass constructor, not when creating the subclass prototype.

Once we've created the SpaceShip prototype object, we can add all the properties that are shared by instances, including a type name for indexing into the scene's table of image data and methods specific to spaceships.

```
SpaceShip.prototype.type = "spaceShip";

SpaceShip.prototype.scorePoint = function() {
    this.points++;
};

SpaceShip.prototype.left = function() {
    this.moveTo(Math.max(this.x - 10, 0), this.y);
};
```

```
SpaceShip.prototype.right = function() {
    var maxWidth = this.scene.width - this.width();
    this.moveTo(Math.min(this.x + 10, maxWidth), this.y);
};
```

Figure 4.7 shows a diagram of the inheritance hierarchy for instances of SpaceShip. Notice how the scene, x, and y properties are defined

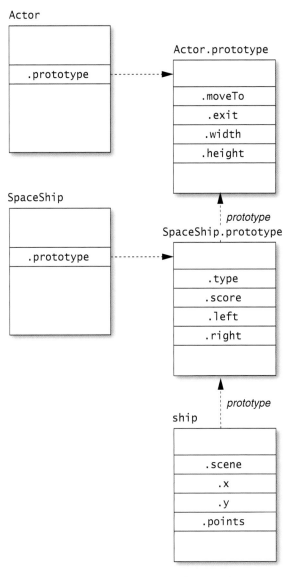

Figure 4.7 An inheritance hierarchy with subclasses

only on the instance object, rather than on any prototype object, despite being created by the `Actor` constructor.

Things to Remember

+ Call the superclass constructor explicitly from subclass constructors, passing `this` as the explicit receiver.

+ Use `Object.create` to construct the subclass prototype object to avoid calling the superclass constructor.

Item 39: Never Reuse Superclass Property Names

Imagine that we wish to add functionality to the scene graph library of Item 38 for collecting diagnostic information, which can be useful for debugging or profiling. To do this, we'd like to give each `Actor` instance a unique identification number:

```
function Actor(scene, x, y) {
    this.scene = scene;
    this.x = x;
    this.y = y;
    this.id = ++Actor.nextID;
    scene.register(this);
}
```

```
Actor.nextID = 0;
```

Now let's do the same thing for individual instances of a subclass of Actor—say, an `Alien` class representing enemies of our spaceship. In addition to its actor identification number, we'd like each alien to have a separate alien identification number.

```
function Alien(scene, x, y, direction, speed, strength) {
    Actor.call(this, scene, x, y);
    this.direction = direction;
    this.speed = speed;
    this.strength = strength;
    this.damage = 0;
    this.id = ++Alien.nextID; // conflicts with actor id!
}
```

```
Alien.nextID = 0;
```

This code creates a conflict between the `Alien` class and its `Actor` superclass: Both classes attempt to write to an instance property called id. While each class may consider the property to be "private" (i.e., only relevant and accessible to methods defined directly on that class), the fact is that the property is stored on instance objects and named with a string. If two classes in an inheritance hierarchy refer to the same property name, they will refer to the same property.

As a result, subclasses must always be aware of all properties used by their superclasses, even if those properties are conceptually private. The obvious resolution in this case is to use distinct property names for the Actor identification number and Alien identification number:

```
function Actor(scene, x, y) {
    this.scene = scene;
    this.x = x;
    this.y = y;
    this.actorID = ++Actor.nextID; // distinct from alienID
    scene.register(this);
}

Actor.nextID = 0;

function Alien(scene, x, y, direction, speed, strength) {
    Actor.call(this, scene, x, y);
    this.direction = direction;
    this.speed = speed;
    this.strength = strength;
    this.damage = 0;
    this.alienID = ++Alien.nextID; // distinct from actorID
}

Alien.nextID = 0;
```

Things to Remember

✦ Be aware of all property names used by your superclasses.

✦ Never reuse a superclass property name in a subclass.

Item 40: Avoid Inheriting from Standard Classes

The ECMAScript standard library is small, but it comes with a handful of important classes such as Array, Function, and Date. It can be tempting to extend these with subclasses, but unfortunately their definitions have enough special behavior that well-behaved subclasses are impossible to write.

A good example is the Array class. A library for operating on file systems might wish to create an abstraction of directories that inherits all of the behavior of arrays:

```
function Dir(path, entries) {
    this.path = path;
    for (var i = 0, n = entries.length; i < n; i++) {
        this[i] = entries[i];
    }
}
```

```
Dir.prototype = Object.create(Array.prototype);
// extends Array
```

Unfortunately, this approach breaks the expected behavior of the length property of arrays:

```
var dir = new Dir("/tmp/mysite",
                   ["index.html", "script.js", "style.css"]);
dir.length; // 0
```

The reason this fails is that the length property operates specially on objects that are marked internally as "true" arrays. The ECMA-Script standard specifies this as an invisible *internal property* called [[Class]]. Don't let the name mislead you—JavaScript doesn't secretly have an internal class system. The value of [[Class]] is just a simple tag: Array objects (created by the Array constructor or the [] syntax) are stamped with the [[Class]] value "Array", functions are stamped with the [[Class]] value "Function", and so on. Table 4.1 shows the complete set of [[Class]] values defined by ECMAScript.

So what does this magic [[Class]] property have to do with length? As it turns out, the behavior of length is defined specially for objects whose [[Class]] internal property has the value "Array". For these objects, the length property keeps itself in sync with the number of indexed properties of the object. If you add more indexed properties to the object, the length property increases itself automatically; if you decrease length, it automatically deletes any indexed properties beyond its new value.

But when we extend the Array class, instances of the subclass are not created by new Array() or the literal [] syntax. So instances of Dir have the [[Class]] "Object". There is even a test for this: The default Object.prototype.toString method queries the internal [[Class]] property of its receiver to create a generic description of an object, so you can call it explicitly on any given object and see:

```
var dir = new Dir("/", []);
Object.prototype.toString.call(dir); // "[object Object]"
Object.prototype.toString.call([]);  // "[object Array]"
```

As a result, instances of Dir do not inherit the expected special behavior of the length property of arrays.

Table 4.1 Values of the [[Class]] Internal Property, As Defined by ECMAScript

[[Class]]	Construction
"Array"	new Array(...), [...]
"Boolean"	new Boolean(...)
"Date"	new Date(...)
"Error"	new Error(...), new EvalError(...), new RangeError(...), new ReferenceError(...), new SyntaxError(...), new TypeError(...), new URIError(...)
"Function"	new Function(...), function(...) {...}
"JSON"	JSON
"Math"	Math
"Number"	new Number(...)
"Object"	new Object(...), {...}, new MyClass(...)
"RegExp"	new RegExp(...), /.../
"String"	new String(...)

A better implementation defines an instance property with the array of entries:

```
function Dir(path, entries) {
    this.path = path;
    this.entries = entries; // array property
}
```

Array methods can be redefined on the prototype by delegating to the corresponding methods of the entries property:

```
Dir.prototype.forEach = function(f, thisArg) {
    if (typeof thisArg === "undefined") {
        thisArg = this;
    }
    this.entries.forEach(f, thisArg);
};
```

Most of the constructors of the ECMAScript standard library have similar problems, where certain properties or methods expect the right [[Class]] or other special internal properties that subclasses cannot provide. For this reason it's advisable to avoid inheriting from any of the following standard classes: Array, Boolean, Date, Function, Number, RegExp, or String.

Things to Remember

✦ Inheriting from standard classes tends to break due to special internal properties such as [[Class]].

✦ Prefer delegating to properties instead of inheriting from standard classes.

Item 41: Treat Prototypes As an Implementation Detail

An object provides a small, simple, and powerful set of operations to its consumers. The most basic interactions a consumer has with an object are getting its property values and calling its methods. These operations do not particularly care where in a prototype hierarchy the properties are stored. The implementation of an object may evolve over time to implement a property in different places on the object's prototype chain, but as long as its value remains consistent, these basic operations behave the same. Put simply: Prototypes are an implementation detail of an object's behavior.

At the same time, JavaScript provides convenient *introspection* mechanisms for inspecting the details of an object. The Object.prototype .hasOwnProperty method determines whether a property is stored directly as an "own" property (i.e., an instance property) of an object, ignoring the prototype hierarchy completely. The Object.getPrototypeOf and __proto__ facilities (see Item 30) allow programs to traverse the prototype chain of an object and look at its prototype objects individually. These are powerful and sometimes useful features.

But a good programmer knows when to respect abstraction boundaries. Inspecting implementation details—even without modifying them—creates a dependency between components of a program. If the producer of an object changes its implementation details, the consumer that depends on them will break. These kinds of bugs can be especially difficult to diagnose because they constitute *action at a distance:* One author changes the implementation of one component, and another component (often written by a different programmer) breaks.

Similarly, JavaScript does not distinguish between public and private properties of an object (see Item 35). Instead, it's your responsibility to rely on documentation and discipline. If a library provides an object with properties that are undocumented or specifically documented as internal, chances are good that those properties are best left alone by consumers.

Things to Remember

✦ Objects are interfaces; prototypes are implementations.

✦ Avoid inspecting the prototype structure of objects you don't control.

✦ Avoid inspecting properties that implement the internals of objects you don't control.

Item 42: Avoid Reckless Monkey-Patching

Having inveighed against violating abstractions in Item 41, let's now consider the ultimate violation. Since prototypes are shared as objects, anyone can add, remove, or modify their properties. This controversial practice is commonly known as *monkey-patching.*

The appeal of monkey-patching lies in its power. Are arrays missing a useful method? Just add it yourself:

```
Array.prototype.split = function(i) { // alternative #1
    return [this.slice(0, i), this.slice(i)];
};
```

Voilà: Every array instance has a split method.

But problems arise when multiple libraries monkey-patch the same prototypes in incompatible ways. Another library might monkey-patch Array.prototype with a method of the same name:

```
Array.prototype.split = function() { // alternative #2
    var i = Math.floor(this.length / 2);
    return [this.slice(0, i), this.slice(i)];
};
```

Any uses of split on an array now have roughly a 50% chance of being broken, depending on which of the two methods they expect.

At the very least, any library that modifies shared prototypes such as Array.prototype should clearly document that it does so. This at least gives clients adequate warning about potential conflicts between libraries. Nevertheless, two libraries that monkey-patch prototypes in conflicting ways cannot be used within the same program. One alternative is that if a library only monkey-patches prototypes as a convenience, it may provide the modifications in a function that users can choose to call or ignore:

```
function addArrayMethods() {
    Array.prototype.split = function(i) {
        return [this.slice(0, i), this.slice(i)];
    };
};
```

Of course, this approach only works if the library providing addArrayMethods does not actually depend on `Array.prototype.split`.

Despite the hazards, there is one particularly reliable and invaluable use of monkey-patching: the *polyfill.* JavaScript programs and libraries are frequently deployed on multiple platforms, such as the different versions of web browsers made by different vendors. These platforms can differ in how many standard APIs they implement. For example, ES5 defines new `Array` methods such as `forEach`, `map`, and `filter`, and some versions of browsers may not support these methods. The behavior of the missing methods is defined by a widely supported standard, and many programs and libraries may depend on these methods. Since their behavior is standardized, providing implementations for these methods does not pose the same risk of incompatibility between libraries. In fact, multiple libraries can provide implementations for the same standard methods (assuming they are all correctly implemented), since they all implement the same standard API.

You can safely fill in these platform gaps by guarding monkey-patches with a test:

```
if (typeof Array.prototype.map !== "function") {
    Array.prototype.map = function(f, thisArg) {
        var result = [];
        for (var i = 0, n = this.length; i < n; i++) {
            result[i] = f.call(thisArg, this[i], i);
        }
        return result;
    };
}
```

Testing for the presence of `Array.prototype.map` ensures that a built-in implementation, which is likely to be more efficient and better tested, won't be overwritten.

Things to Remember

✦ Avoid reckless monkey-patching.

✦ Document any monkey-patching performed by a library.

✦ Consider making monkey-patching optional by performing the modifications in an exported function.

✦ Use monkey-patching to provide polyfills for missing standard APIs.

5

Arrays and Dictionaries

Objects are JavaScript's most versatile data structure. Depending on the situation, an object can represent a fixed record of name-value associations, an object-oriented data abstraction with inherited methods, a dense or sparse array, or a hash table. Naturally, mastering such a multipurpose tool demands different idioms for different needs. In the preceding chapter we studied the use of structured objects and inheritance. This chapter tackles the use of objects as *collections:* aggregate data structures with varying numbers of elements.

Item 43: Build Lightweight Dictionaries from Direct Instances of Object

At its heart, a JavaScript object is a table mapping string property names to values. This makes objects pleasantly lightweight for implementing *dictionaries:* variable-sized collections mapping strings to values. JavaScript even provides a convenient construct for enumerating the property names of an object, the for...in loop:

```
var dict = { alice: 34, bob: 24, chris: 62 };
var people = [];

for (var name in dict) {
    people.push(name + ": " + dict[name]);
}

people; // ["alice: 34", "bob: 24", "chris: 62"]
```

But every object also inherits properties from its prototype object (see Chapter 4), and the for...in loop enumerates an object's inherited properties as well as its "own" properties. For example, what happens if we create a custom dictionary class that stores its elements as properties of the dictionary object itself?

```javascript
function NaiveDict() { }

NaiveDict.prototype.count = function() {
    var i = 0;
    for (var name in this) { // counts every property
        i++;
    }
    return i;
};

NaiveDict.prototype.toString = function() {
    return "[object NaiveDict]";
};

var dict = new NaiveDict();

dict.alice = 34;
dict.bob = 24;
dict.chris = 62;

dict.count(); // 5
```

The problem is that we are using the same object to store both the fixed properties of the NaiveDict data structure (count, toString) and the variable entries of the specific dictionary (alice, bob, chris). So when count enumerates the properties of a dictionary, it counts all of these properties (count, toString, alice, bob, chris) instead of just the entries we care about. See Item 45 for an improved Dict class that does not store its elements as instance properties, instead providing dict.get(key) and dict.set(key, value) methods. In this Item we focus on the pattern of using object properties as dictionary elements.

A similar mistake is to use the Array type to represent dictionaries. This is an especially easy trap to fall into for programmers familiar with languages such as Perl and PHP, where dictionaries are commonly called "associative arrays." Deceptively, since we can add properties to any type of JavaScript object this usage pattern will *sometimes* appear to work:

```javascript
var dict = new Array();

dict.alice = 34;
dict.bob = 24;
dict.chris = 62;

dict.bob; // 24
```

Unfortunately, this code is vulnerable to *prototype pollution*, where properties on a prototype object can cause unexpected properties to appear when enumerating dictionary entries. For example, another library in the application may decide to add some convenience methods to Array.prototype:

```
Array.prototype.first = function() {
    return this[0];
};

Array.prototype.last = function() {
    return this[this.length - 1];
};
```

Now see what happens when we attempt to enumerate the elements of our array:

```
var names = [];

for (var name in dict) {
    names.push(name);
}

names; // ["alice", "bob", "chris", "first", "last"]
```

This brings us to the primary rule of using objects as lightweight dictionaries: Only use direct instances of Object as dictionaries—not subclasses such as NaiveDict, and certainly not arrays. For example, we can simply replace new Array() above with new Object() or even an empty object literal. The result is much less susceptible to prototype pollution:

```
var dict = {};

dict.alice = 34;
dict.bob = 24;
dict.chris = 62;

var names = [];

for (var name in dict) {
    names.push(name);
}

names; // ["alice", "bob", "chris"]
```

Now, our new version is still not guaranteed to be safe from pollution. Anyone could still come along and add properties to Object.prototype, and we'd be stuck again. But by using a direct instance of Object, we localize the risk to Object.prototype alone.

So how is this solution any better? For one, as Item 47 explains, nobody should *ever* add properties to Object.prototype that could pollute a for...in loop. By contrast, it's not unreasonable to add properties to Array.prototype. For example, Item 42 explains how to add standard methods to Array.prototype in environments that don't provide them. These properties end up polluting for...in loops. Similarly, a user-defined class will typically have properties on its prototype. Sticking to direct instances of Object (and always observing the rule of Item 47) keeps your for...in loops free of pollution.

But beware! As Items 44 and 45 attest, this rule is necessary but not sufficient for building well-behaved dictionaries. As convenient as lightweight dictionaries are, they suffer from a number of hazards. It's important to study all three of these Items—or, if you prefer not to memorize the rules, use an abstraction like the Dict class of Item 45.

Things to Remember

◆ Use object literals to construct lightweight dictionaries.

◆ Lightweight dictionaries should be direct descendants of Object.prototype to protect against prototype pollution in for...in loops.

Item 44: Use null Prototypes to Prevent Prototype Pollution

One of the easiest ways to avoid prototype pollution is to just make it impossible in the first place. But before ES5, there was no standard way to create a new object with an empty prototype. You might be tempted to try setting a constructor's prototype property to null or undefined:

```
function C() { }
C.prototype = null;
```

But instantiating this constructor still results in instances of Object:

```
var o = new C();
Object.getPrototypeOf(o) === null;                // false
Object.getPrototypeOf(o) === Object.prototype;    // true
```

ES5 offers the first standard way to create an object with no prototype. The Object.create function is capable of dynamically constructing objects with a user-specified prototype link and a *property descriptor map,* which describes the values and attributes of the new object's properties. By simply passing a null prototype argument and an empty descriptor map, we can build a truly empty object:

```
var x = Object.create(null);
Object.getPrototypeOf(x) === null;    // true
```

No amount of prototype pollution can affect the behavior of such an object.

Older JavaScript environments that do not support Object.create may support one other approach worth mentioning. In many environments, the special property __proto__ (see Items 31 and 32) provides magic read and write access to the internal prototype link of an object. The object literal syntax also supports initializing the prototype link of a new object to null:

```
var x = { __proto__: null };
x instanceof Object;                  // false (non-standard)
```

This syntax is equally convenient, but where Object.create is available, it is the more reliable approach. The __proto__ property is nonstandard and not all uses of it are portable. JavaScript implementations are not guaranteed to support it in the future, so you should stick to the standard Object.create where possible.

Sadly, while the nonstandard __proto__ can be used to solve some problems, it also *causes* an additional problem of its own, preventing prototype-free objects from being a truly robust implementation of dictionaries. Item 45 describes how in some JavaScript environments, the property key "__proto__" itself pollutes objects *even when they have no prototype.* If you can't be sure that the string "__proto__" will never be used as a key in your dictionary, you should consider using the more robust Dict class described in Item 45.

Things to Remember

+ In ES5, use Object.create(null) to create prototype-free empty objects that are less susceptible to pollution.

+ In older environments, consider using { __proto__: null }.

+ But beware that __proto__ is neither standard nor entirely portable and may be removed in future JavaScript environments.

+ Never use the name "__proto__" as a dictionary key since some environments treat this property specially.

Item 45: Use `hasOwnProperty` to Protect Against Prototype Pollution

Items 43 and 44 talk about property *enumeration*, but we haven't addressed the issue of prototype pollution in property *lookup*. It's tempting to use JavaScript's native syntax for object manipulation for all of our dictionary operations:

```
"alice" in dict;    // membership test
dict.alice;         // retrieval
dict.alice = 24;    // update
```

But remember that JavaScript's object operations always work with inheritance. Even an empty object literal inherits a number of properties from `Object.prototype`:

```
var dict = {};
```

```
"alice" in dict;        // false
"bob" in dict;          // false
"chris" in dict;        // false
"toString" in dict;     // true
"valueOf" in dict;      // true
```

Luckily, `Object.prototype` provides the `hasOwnProperty` method, which is just the tool we need to avoid prototype pollution when testing for dictionary entries:

```
dict.hasOwnProperty("alice");    // false
dict.hasOwnProperty("toString"); // false
dict.hasOwnProperty("valueOf");  // false
```

Similarly, we can protect property lookups against pollution by guarding the lookup with a test:

```
dict.hasOwnProperty("alice") ? dict.alice : undefined;
dict.hasOwnProperty(x) ? dict[x] : undefined;
```

Unfortunately, we aren't quite done. When we call `dict.hasOwnProperty`, we're asking to look up the `hasOwnProperty` method of `dict`. Normally this would simply be inherited from `Object.prototype`. But if we store an entry in the dictionary under the name `"hasOwnProperty"`, the prototype's method is no longer accessible:

```
dict.hasOwnProperty = 10;
dict.hasOwnProperty("alice");
// error: dict.hasOwnProperty is not a function
```

You might be thinking that a dictionary would never store an entry with a name as exotic as `"hasOwnProperty"`. And of course, it's up to you in the context of any given program to decide that this isn't a scenario you ever expect to happen. But it certainly can happen, especially if you're filling the dictionary with entries from an external file, network resource, or user interface input, where third parties beyond your control get to decide what keys end up in the dictionary.

The safest approach is to make no assumptions. Instead of calling hasOwnProperty as a method of the dictionary, we can use the call method described in Item 20. First we extract the hasOwnProperty method in advance from any well-known location:

```
var hasOwn = Object.prototype.hasOwnProperty;
```

Or more concisely:

```
var hasOwn = {}.hasOwnProperty;
```

Now that we have a local variable bound to the proper function, we can call it on any object by using the function's call method:

```
hasOwn.call(dict, "alice");
```

This approach works regardless of whether its receiver has overridden its hasOwnProperty method:

```
var dict = {};

dict.alice = 24;
hasOwn.call(dict, "hasOwnProperty"); // false
hasOwn.call(dict, "alice");          // true

dict.hasOwnProperty = 10;
hasOwn.call(dict, "hasOwnProperty"); // true
hasOwn.call(dict, "alice");          // true
```

To avoid inserting this boilerplate everywhere we do a lookup, we can abstract out this pattern into a Dict constructor that encapsulates all of the techniques for writing robust dictionaries in a single datatype definition:

```
function Dict(elements) {
    // allow an optional initial table
    this.elements = elements || {};    // simple Object
}

Dict.prototype.has = function(key) {
    // own property only
    return {}.hasOwnProperty.call(this.elements, key);
};
```

```
Dict.prototype.get = function(key) {
    // own property only
    return this.has(key)
        ? this.elements[key]
        : undefined;
};
```

```
Dict.prototype.set = function(key, val) {
    this.elements[key] = val;
};
```

```
Dict.prototype.remove = function(key) {
    delete this.elements[key];
};
```

Notice that we don't protect the implementation of Dict.prototype.set, since adding the key to the dictionary object becomes one of the elements object's own properties, even if there is a property of the same name in Object.prototype.

This abstraction is more robust than using JavaScript's default object syntax and almost as convenient to use:

```
var dict = new Dict({
    alice: 34,
    bob: 24,
    chris: 62
});
```

```
dict.has("alice");    // true
dict.get("bob");      // 24
dict.has("valueOf");  // false
```

Recall from Item 44 that in some JavaScript environments, the special property name __proto__ can cause pollution problems of its own. In some environments, the __proto__ property is simply inherited from Object.prototype, so empty objects are (mercifully) truly empty:

```
var empty = Object.create(null);
"__proto__" in empty;
// false (in some environments)
```

```
var hasOwn = {}.hasOwnProperty;
hasOwn.call(empty, "__proto__");
// false (in some environments)
```

In others, only the `in` operator reports true:

```
var empty = Object.create(null);
"__proto__" in empty;              // true (in some environments)

var hasOwn = {}.hasOwnProperty;
hasOwn.call(empty, "__proto__"); // false (in some
environments)
```

But unfortunately, some environments permanently pollute all objects with the appearance of an instance property called __proto__:

```
var empty = Object.create(null);
"__proto__" in empty;              // true (in some environments)

var hasOwn = {}.hasOwnProperty;
hasOwn.call(empty, "__proto__"); // true (in some environments)
```

This means that depending on the environment, the following code could have different results:

```
var dict = new Dict();
dict.has("__proto__"); // ?
```

For maximum portability and safety, this leaves us with no choice but to add a special case for the `"__proto__"` key to each of the `Dict` methods, resulting in the following more complex but safer final implementation:

```
function Dict(elements) {
    // allow an optional initial table
    this.elements = elements || {};      // simple Object
    this.hasSpecialProto = false;        // has "__proto__" key?
    this.specialProto = undefined;       // "__proto__" element
}

Dict.prototype.has = function(key) {
    if (key === "__proto__") {
        return this.hasSpecialProto;
    }
    // own property only
    return {}.hasOwnProperty.call(this.elements, key);
};

Dict.prototype.get = function(key) {
    if (key === "__proto__") {
        return this.specialProto;
    }
```

```
    // own property only
    return this.has(key)
        ? this.elements[key]
        : undefined;
};

Dict.prototype.set = function(key, val) {
    if (key === "__proto__") {
        this.hasSpecialProto = true;
        this.specialProto = val;
    } else {
        this.elements[key] = val;
    }
};

Dict.prototype.remove = function(key) {
    if (key === "__proto__") {
        this.hasSpecialProto = false;
        this.specialProto = undefined;
    } else {
        delete this.elements[key];
    }
};
```

This implementation is guaranteed to work regardless of an environment's handling of __proto__, since it avoids ever dealing with properties of that name:

```
var dict = new Dict();
dict.has("__proto__"); // false
```

Things to Remember

✦ Use hasOwnProperty to protect against prototype pollution.

✦ Use lexical scope and call to protect against overriding of the hasOwnProperty method.

✦ Consider implementing dictionary operations in a class that encapsulates the boilerplate hasOwnProperty tests.

✦ Use a dictionary class to protect against the use of "__proto__" as a key.

Item 46: Prefer Arrays to Dictionaries for Ordered Collections

Intuitively, a JavaScript object is an unordered collection of proper-ties. Getting and setting different properties should work in any order, producing the same results and roughly the same efficiency. The ECMAScript standard does not specify any particular order of prop-erty storage and is even largely mum on the subject of enumeration.

But here's the catch: A for...in loop has to pick *some* order to enu-merate an object's properties. And since the standard allows Java-Script engines the freedom to choose an order, their choice can subtly change your program's behavior. A common mistake is to provide an API that requires an object representing an ordered mapping from strings to values, such as for creating an ordered report:

```
function report(highScores) {
    var result = "";
    var i = 1;
    for (var name in highScores) { // unpredictable order
        result += i + ". " + name + ": " +
                    highScores[name] + "\n";
        i++;
    }
    return result;
}

report({ Hank: 1110100,
         Steve: 1064500,
         Billy: 1050200 });
// ?
```

Because different environments may choose to store and enumer-ate the properties of the object in different orders, this function can result in different strings, potentially jumbling the order of the "high scores" report.

Keep in mind that it may not always be obvious whether your pro-gram depends on the order of object enumeration. If you don't test your program in multiple JavaScript environments, you may not even notice that its behavior can change based on the exact ordering of a for...in loop.

If you need to depend on the order of entries in a data structure, use an array instead of a dictionary. The report function above would work completely predictably in any JavaScript environment if its API expected an array of objects instead of a single object:

```javascript
function report(highScores) {
    var result = "";
    for (var i = 0, n = highScores.length; i < n; i++) {
        var score = highScores[i];
        result += (i + 1) + ". " +
                score.name + ": " + score.points + "\n";
    }
    return result;
}
```

```javascript
report([{ name: "Hank", points: 1110100 },
        { name: "Steve", points: 1064500 },
        { name: "Billy", points: 1050200 }]);
// "1. Hank: 1110100\n2. Steve: 1064500\n3. Billy: 1050200\n"
```

By accepting an array of objects, each with a name and points property, this version predictably iterates over the elements in a precise order: from 0 to highScores.length − 1.

A terrific source of subtle order dependencies is floating-point arithmetic. Consider a dictionary of films that maps titles to ratings:

```javascript
var ratings = {
    "Good Will Hunting": 0.8,
    "Mystic River": 0.7,
    "21": 0.6,
    "Doubt": 0.9
};
```

As we saw in Item 2, rounding in floating-point arithmetic can lead to subtle dependencies on the order of operations. When combined with undefined order of enumeration, this can lead to some unpredictable loops:

```javascript
var total = 0, count = 0;
for (var key in ratings) { // unpredictable order
    total += ratings[key];
    count++;
}
total /= count;
total; // ?
```

As it turns out, popular JavaScript environments do in fact perform this loop in different orders. For example, some environments enumerate object keys in the order in which they are added to the object, effectively computing:

```
(0.8 + 0.7 + 0.6 + 0.9) / 4     // 0.75
```

Others always enumerate potential array indices first before any other keys. Since the movie *21* happens to have a name that is a viable array index, it gets enumerated first, resulting in:

```
(0.6 + 0.8 + 0.7 + 0.9) / 4     // 0.7499999999999999
```

In this case, a better representation is to use integer values in the dictionary, since integer addition can be performed in any order. This way, the sensitive division operations are performed only at the very end—crucially, after the loop is complete:

```
(8 + 7 + 6 + 9) / 4 / 10     // 0.75
(6 + 8 + 7 + 9) / 4 / 10     // 0.75
```

In general, you should always take care when executing a for...in loop that the operations you perform behave the same regardless of their order.

Things to Remember

+ Avoid relying on the order in which for...in loops enumerate object properties.

+ If you aggregate data in a dictionary, make sure the aggregate operations are order-insensitive.

+ Use arrays instead of dictionary objects for ordered collections.

Item 47: Never Add Enumerable Properties to `Object.prototype`

The for...in loop is awfully convenient, but as we saw in Item 43 it is susceptible to prototype pollution. Now, the most common use of for...in by far is enumerating the elements of a dictionary. The implication is unavoidable: If you want to permit the use of for...in on dictionary objects, never add enumerable properties to the shared `Object.prototype`.

This rule may come as a great disappointment: What could be more powerful than adding convenience methods to `Object.prototype` that suddenly all objects can share? For example, what if we added an `allKeys` method that produces an array of an object's property names?

```
Object.prototype.allKeys = function() {
    var result = [];
    for (var key in this) {
        result.push(key);
    }
    return result;
};
```

Sadly, this method pollutes even its own result:

```
({ a: 1, b: 2, c: 3 }).allKeys(); // ["allKeys", "a", "b", "c"]
```

Of course, we could always improve our allKeys method to ignore properties of Object.prototype. But with freedom comes responsibility, and our actions on a highly shared prototype object have consequences on everyone who uses that object. Just by adding one single property to Object.prototype, we force *everyone everywhere* to protect his for...in loops.

It is slightly less convenient, but ultimately much more cooperative, to define allKeys as a function rather than as a method.

```
function allKeys(obj) {
    var result = [];
    for (var key in obj) {
        result.push(key);
    }
    return result;
}
```

But if you do want to add properties to Object.prototype, ES5 provides a mechanism for doing it more cooperatively. The Object.defineProperty method makes it possible to define an object property simultaneously with metadata about the property's *attributes.* For example, we can define the above property exactly as before but make it invisible to for...in by setting its enumerable attribute to false:

```
Object.defineProperty(Object.prototype, "allKeys", {
    value: function() {
        var result = [];
        for (var key in this) {
            result.push(key);
        }
        return result;
    },
    writable: true,
```

```
    enumerable: false,
    configurable: true
});
```

Admittedly, this code is a mouthful. But this version has the distinct advantage of not polluting every other for...in loop over every other instance of Object.

In fact, it's worth using this technique for other objects as well. Whenever you need to add a property that should not be visible to for...in loops, Object.defineProperty is your friend.

Things to Remember

✦ Avoid adding properties to Object.prototype.

✦ Consider writing a function instead of an Object.prototype method.

✦ If you do add properties to Object.prototype, use ES5's Object.defineProperty to define them as nonenumerable properties.

Item 48: Avoid Modifying an Object during Enumeration

A social network has a set of members and, for each member, a registered list of friends:

```
function Member(name) {
    this.name = name;
    this.friends = [];
}

var a = new Member("Alice"),
    b = new Member("Bob"),
    c = new Member("Carol"),
    d = new Member("Dieter"),
    e = new Member("Eli"),
    f = new Member("Fatima");

a.friends.push(b);
b.friends.push(c);
c.friends.push(e);
d.friends.push(b);
e.friends.push(d, f);
```

Searching that network means traversing the social network graph (see Figure 5.1). This is often implemented with a work-set, which

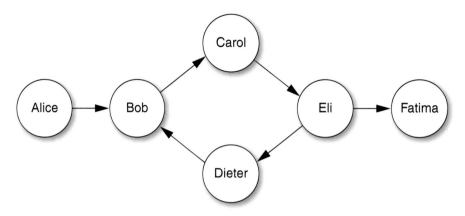

Figure 5.1 A social network graph

starts with a single root node, and has nodes added as they are discovered and removed as they are visited. It may be tempting to try to
implement this traversal with a single for...in loop:

```
Member.prototype.inNetwork = function(other) {
    var visited = {};
    var workset = {};

    workset[this.name] = this;

    for (var name in workset) {
        var member = workset[name];
        delete workset[name];    // modified while enumerating
        if (name in visited) {   // don't revisit members
            continue;
        }
        visited[name] = member;
        if (member === other) { // found?
            return true;
        }
        member.friends.forEach(function(friend) {
            workset[friend.name] = friend;
        });
    }

    return false;
};
```

Unfortunately, in many JavaScript environments this code doesn't work at all:

```
a.inNetwork(f); // false
```

What happened? As it turns out, a for...in loop is not required to keep current with modifications to the object being enumerated. In fact, the ECMAScript standard leaves room for different JavaScript environments to behave differently with respect to concurrent modifications. In particular, the standard states:

> If new properties are added to the object being enumerated during enumeration, the newly added properties are not guaranteed to be visited in the active enumeration.

The practical consequence of this underspecification is that we cannot rely on for...in loops to behave predictably if we modify the object being enumerated.

Let's give our graph traversal another try, this time managing the loop control ourselves. While we're at it, we should use our dictionary abstraction to avoid prototype pollution. We can place the dictionary in a WorkSet class that tracks the number of elements currently in the set:

```
function WorkSet() {
    this.entries = new Dict();
    this.count = 0;
}

WorkSet.prototype.isEmpty = function() {
    return this.count === 0;
};

WorkSet.prototype.add = function(key, val) {
    if (this.entries.has(key)) {
        return;
    }
    this.entries.set(key, val);
    this.count++;
};

WorkSet.prototype.get = function(key) {
    return this.entries.get(key);
};

WorkSet.prototype.remove = function(key) {
    if (!this.entries.has(key)) {
```

```
        return;
    }
    this.entries.remove(key);
    this.count--;
};
```

In order to pick an arbitrary element of the set, we need a new method for the Dict class:

```
Dict.prototype.pick = function() {
    for (var key in this.elements) {
        if (this.has(key)) {
            return key;
        }
    }
    throw new Error("empty dictionary");
};


WorkSet.prototype.pick = function() {
    return this.entries.pick();
};
```

Now we can implement inNetwork with a simple while loop, choosing arbitrary elements one at a time and removing them from the work-set.

```
Member.prototype.inNetwork = function(other) {
    var visited = {};
    var workset = new WorkSet();
    workset.add(this.name, this);
    while (!workset.isEmpty()) {
        var name = workset.pick();
        var member = workset.get(name);
        workset.remove(name);
        if (name in visited) { // don't revisit members
            continue;
        }
        visited[name] = member;
        if (member === other) { // found?
            return true;
        }
        member.friends.forEach(function(friend) {
            workset.add(friend.name, friend);
        });
    }
    return false;
};
```

The pick method is an example of *nondeterminism:* an operation that is not guaranteed by the language semantics to produce a single, pre-dictable result. This nondeterminism comes from the fact that the for...in loop may choose a different order of enumeration in different JavaScript environments (or even in different executions within the same JavaScript environment, at least in principle). Working with nondeterminism can be tricky, because it introduces an element of unpredictability into your program. Tests that pass on one platform may fail on others or even fail intermittently on the same platform.

Some sources of nondeterminism are unavoidable. A random num-ber generator is *supposed* to produce unpredictable results; checking the current date and time always gets a different answer; respond-ing to user actions such as mouse clicks or keystrokes necessarily behaves differently depending on the user. But it's a good idea to be clear about what parts of a program have a single expected result and which parts can vary.

For these reasons, it's worth considering using a deterministic alter-native to a work-set algorithm: a work-list algorithm. By storing work items in an array instead of a set, the inNetwork method always tra-verses the graph in exactly the same order.

```
Member.prototype.inNetwork = function(other) {
    var visited = {};
    var worklist = [this];
    while (worklist.length > 0) {
        var member = worklist.pop();
        if (member.name in visited) {    // don't revisit
            continue;
        }
        visited[member.name] = member;
        if (member === other) {          // found?
            return true;
        }
        member.friends.forEach(function(friend) {
            worklist.push(friend);       // add to work-list
        });
    }
    return false;
};
```

This version of inNetwork adds and removes work items deterministi-cally. Since the method always returns true for connected members no matter what path it finds, the end result is the same. But this may not be the case for other methods you might care to write, such as a variation on inNetwork that produces the actual path found through the graph from member to member.

Things to Remember

✦ Make sure not to modify an object while enumerating its properties with a for...in loop.

✦ Use a while loop or classic for loop instead of a for...in loop when iterating over an object whose contents might change during the loop.

✦ For predictable enumeration over a changing data structure, consider using a sequential data structure such as an array instead of a dictionary object.

Item 49: **Prefer** for **Loops to** for...in **Loops for Array Iteration**

What is the value of mean in this code?

```
var scores = [98, 74, 85, 77, 93, 100, 89];
var total = 0;
for (var score in scores) {
    total += score;
}
var mean = total / scores.length;
mean; // ?
```

Did you spot the bug? If you said the answer was 88, you understood the intention of the program but not its actual result. This program commits the all-too-easy mistake of confusing the *keys* and *values* of an array of numbers. A for...in loop always enumerates the keys. A plausible next guess would be (0 + 1 + ... + 6) / 7 = 21, but even that is incorrect. Remember that object property keys are always strings, even the indexed properties of an array. So the += operation ends up performing string concatenation, resulting in an unintended total of "00123456". The end result? An implausible mean value of 17636.571428571428.

The proper way to iterate over the contents of an array is to use a classic for loop.

```
var scores = [98, 74, 85, 77, 93, 100, 89];
var total = 0;
for (var i = 0, n = scores.length; i < n; i++) {
    total += scores[i];
}
```

```
var mean = total / scores.length;
mean; // 88
```

This approach ensures that you have integer indices when you need them and array element values when you need them, and that you never confuse the two or trigger unexpected coercions to strings. Moreover, it ensures that the iteration occurs in the proper order and does not accidentally include noninteger properties stored on the array object or in its prototype chain.

Notice the use of the array length variable n in the for loop above. If the loop body does not modify the array, the loop behavior is identical to simply recalculating the array length on every iteration:

```
for (var i = 0; i < scores.length; i++) { ... }
```

Still, there are a couple of small benefits to computing the array length once ahead of the loop. First, even optimizing JavaScript compilers may sometimes find it difficult to prove that it is safe to avoid recomputing scores.length. But more importantly, it communicates to the person reading the code that the loop's termination condition is simple and fixed.

Things to Remember

- Always use a for loop rather than a for...in loop for iterating over the indexed properties of an array.

- Consider storing the length property of an array in a local variable before a loop to avoid recomputing the property lookup.

Item 50: Prefer Iteration Methods to Loops

Good programmers hate writing the same code twice. Copying and pasting boilerplate code duplicates bugs, makes programs harder to change, clutters up programs with repetitive patterns, and leaves programmers endlessly reinventing the wheel. Perhaps worst of all, repetition makes it too easy for someone reading a program to overlook minor differences from one instance of a pattern to another.

JavaScript's for loops are reasonably concise and certainly familiar from many other languages such as C, Java, and C#, but they allow for quite different behavior with only slight syntactic variation. Some of the most notorious bugs in programming result from simple mistakes in determining the termination condition of a loop:

```
for (var i = 0; i <= n; i++) { ... }
// extra end iteration
for (var i = 1; i < n; i++) { ... }
// missing first iteration
```

```
for (var i = n; i >= 0; i--) { ... }
// extra start iteration
for (var i = n - 1; i > 0; i--) { ... }
// missing last iteration
```

Let's face it: Figuring out termination conditions is a drag. It's boring and there are just too many little ways to mess up.

Thankfully, JavaScript's closures (see Item 11) are a convenient and expressive way to build iteration abstractions for these patterns that save us from having to copy and paste loop headers.

ES5 provides convenience methods for some of the most common patterns. `Array.prototype.forEach` is the simplest of these. Instead of writing:

```
for (var i = 0, n = players.length; i < n; i++) {
    players[i].score++;
}
```

we can write:

```
players.forEach(function(p) {
    p.score++;
});
```

This code is not only more concise and readable, but it also eliminates the termination condition *and* any mention of array indices.

Another common pattern is to build a new array by doing something to each element of another array. We could do this with a loop:

```
var trimmed = [];
for (var i = 0, n = input.length; i < n; i++) {
    trimmed.push(input[i].trim());
}
```

Alternatively, we could do this with `forEach`:

```
var trimmed = [];
input.forEach(function(s) {
    trimmed.push(s.trim());
});
```

But this pattern of building a new array from an existing array is so common that ES5 introduced `Array.prototype.map` to make it simpler and more elegant:

```
var trimmed = input.map(function(s) {
    return s.trim();
});
```

Another common pattern is to compute a new array containing only some of the elements of an existing array. Array.prototype.filter makes this straightforward: It takes a *predicate*—a function that produces a truthy value if the element should be kept in the new array, and a falsy value if the element should be dropped. For example, we can extract from a price list only those listings that fall within a particular price range:

```
listings.filter(function(listing) {
    return listing.price >= min && listing.price <= max;
});
```

Of course, these are just methods available by default in ES5. There's nothing stopping us from defining our own iteration abstractions. For example, one pattern that sometimes comes up is extracting the longest prefix of an array that satisfies a predicate:

```
function takeWhile(a, pred) {
    var result = [];
    for (var i = 0, n = a.length; i < n; i++) {
        if (!pred(a[i], i)) {
            break;
        }
        result[i] = a[i];
    }
    return result;
}

var prefix = takeWhile([1, 2, 4, 8, 16, 32], function(n) {
    return n < 10;
}); // [1, 2, 4, 8]
```

Notice that we pass the array index i to pred, which it can choose to use or ignore. In fact, all of the iteration functions in the standard library, including forEach, map, and filter, pass the array index to the user-provided function.

We could also define takeWhile as a method by adding it to Array.prototype (see Item 42 for a discussion of the consequences of monkey-patching standard prototypes like Array.prototype):

```
Array.prototype.takeWhile = function(pred) {
    var result = [];
    for (var i = 0, n = this.length; i < n; i++) {
        if (!pred(this[i], i)) {
            break;
        }
```

```
        result[i] = this[i];
    }
    return result;
};

var prefix = [1, 2, 4, 8, 16, 32].takeWhile(function(n) {
    return n < 10;
}); // [1, 2, 4, 8]
```

There is one thing that loops tend to do better than iteration functions: abnormal control flow operations such as break and continue. For example, it would be awkward to attempt to implement takeWhile using forEach:

```
function takeWhile(a, pred) {
    var result = [];
    a.forEach(function(x, i) {
        if (!pred(x)) {
            // ?
        }
        result[i] = x;
    });
    return result;
}
```

We could use an internal exception to implement the early termination of the loop, but this would be awkward and likely inefficient:

```
function takeWhile(a, pred) {
    var result = [];
    var earlyExit = {}; // unique value signaling loop break
    try {
        a.forEach(function(x, i) {
            if (!pred(x)) {
                throw earlyExit;
            }
            result[i] = x;
        });
    } catch (e) {
        if (e !== earlyExit) { // only catch earlyExit
            throw e;
        }
    }
    return result;
}
```

Once an abstraction becomes more verbose than the code it is replacing, it's a pretty sure sign that the cure is worse than the disease.

Alternatively, the ES5 array methods some and every can be used as loops that may terminate early. Arguably, these methods were not created for this purpose; they are described as predicates, applying a callback predicate repeatedly to each element of an array. Specifically, the some method returns a boolean indicating whether its callback returns a truthy value for any one of the array elements:

```
[1, 10, 100].some(function(x) { return x > 5; }); // true
[1, 10, 100].some(function(x) { return x < 0; }); // false
```

Analogously, every returns a boolean indicating whether its callback returns a truthy value for all of the elements:

```
[1, 2, 3, 4, 5].every(function(x) { return x > 0; }); // true
[1, 2, 3, 4, 5].every(function(x) { return x < 3; }); // false
```

Both methods are *short-circuiting:* If the callback to some ever produces a truthy value, some returns without processing any more elements; similarly, every returns immediately if its callback produces a falsy value.

This behavior makes these methods useful as a variant of forEach that can terminate early. For example, we can implement takeWhile with every:

```
function takeWhile(a, pred) {
    var result = [];
    a.every(function(x, i) {
        if (!pred(x)) {
            return false; // break
        }
        result[i] = x;
        return true; // continue
    });
    return result;
}
```

Things to Remember

✦ Use iteration methods such as Array.prototype.forEach and Array.prototype.map in place of for loops to make code more readable and avoid duplicating loop control logic.

✦ Use custom iteration functions to abstract common loop patterns that are not provided by the standard library.

✦ Traditional loops can still be appropriate in cases where early exit is necessary; alternatively, the some and every methods can be used for early exit.

Item 51: Reuse Generic Array Methods on Array-Like Objects

The standard methods of Array.prototype were designed to be reusable as methods of other objects—even objects that do not inherit from Array. As it turns out, a number of such array-like objects crop up in various places in JavaScript.

A good example is a function's arguments object, described in Item 22. Unfortunately, the arguments object does not inherit from Array.prototype, so we cannot simply call arguments.forEach to iterate over each argument. Instead, we have to extract a reference to the forEach method object and use its call method (see Item 20):

```
function highlight() {
    [].forEach.call(arguments, function(widget) {
        widget.setBackground("yellow");
    });
}
```

The forEach method is a Function object, which means it inherits the call method from Function.prototype. This lets us call forEach with a custom value for its internal binding of this (in our case, the arguments object), followed by any number of arguments (in our case, the single callback function). In other words, this code behaves just like we want.

On the web platform, the DOM's NodeList class is another instance of an array-like object. Operations such as document.getElementsByTagName that query a web page for nodes produce their search results as NodeLists. Like the arguments object, a NodeList acts like an array but does not inherit from Array.prototype.

So what exactly makes an object "array-like"? The basic contract of an array object amounts to two simple rules.

- It has an integer length property in the range $0...2^{32} - 1$.

- The length property is greater than the largest *index* of the object. An index is an integer in the range $0...2^{32} - 2$ whose string representation is the key of a property of the object.

This is all the behavior an object needs to implement to be compatible with any of the methods of Array.prototype. Even a simple object literal can be used to create an array-like object:

```
var arrayLike = { 0: "a", 1: "b", 2: "c", length: 3 };
var result = Array.prototype.map.call(arrayLike, function(s) {
    return s.toUpperCase();
}); // ["A", "B", "C"]
```

Strings act like immutable arrays, too, since they can be indexed and their length can be accessed as a length property. So the Array.prototype methods that do not modify their array work with strings:

```
var result = Array.prototype.map.call("abc", function(s) {
    return s.toUpperCase();
}); // ["A", "B", "C"]
```

Now, simulating *all* the behavior of a JavaScript array is trickier, thanks to two more aspects of the behavior of arrays.

- Setting the length property to a smaller value *n* automatically deletes any properties with an index greater than or equal to *n*.

- Adding a property with an index *n* that is greater than or equal to the value of the length property automatically sets the length property to $n + 1$.

The second of these rules is a particularly tall order, since it requires monitoring the addition of indexed properties in order to update length automatically. Thankfully, neither of these two rules is necessary for the purpose of using Array.prototype methods, since they all forcibly update the length property whenever they add or remove indexed properties.

There is just one Array method that is not fully generic: the array concatenation method concat. This method can be called on any array-like receiver, but it tests the [[Class]] of its arguments. If an argument is a true array, its contents are concatenated to the result; otherwise, the argument is added as a single element. This means, for example, that we can't simply concatenate an array with the contents of an arguments object:

```
function namesColumn() {
    return ["Names"].concat(arguments);
}
namesColumn("Alice", "Bob", "Chris");
// ["Names", { 0: "Alice", 1: "Bob", 2: "Chris" }]
```

In order to convince concat to treat an array-like object as a true array, we have to convert it ourselves. A popular and concise idiom for doing this conversion is to call the slice method on the array-like object:

```
function namesColumn() {
    return ["Names"].concat([].slice.call(arguments));
}
namesColumn("Alice", "Bob", "Chris");
// ["Names", "Alice", "Bob", "Chris"]
```

Things to Remember

✦ Reuse generic Array methods on array-like objects by extracting method objects and using their call method.

✦ Any object can be used with generic Array methods if it has indexed properties and an appropriate length property.

Item 52: Prefer Array Literals to the Array Constructor

JavaScript's elegance owes a lot to its concise literal syntax for the most common building blocks of JavaScript programs: objects, functions, and arrays. A literal is a lovely way to express an array:

```
var a = [1, 2, 3, 4, 5];
```

Now, you could use the Array constructor instead:

```
var a = new Array(1, 2, 3, 4, 5);
```

But even setting aside aesthetics, it turns out that the Array constructor has some subtle issues. For one, you have to be sure that no one has rebound the Array variable:

```
function f(Array) {
    return new Array(1, 2, 3, 4, 5);
}
f(String); // new String(1)
```

You also have to be sure that no one has modified the global Array variable:

```
Array = String;
new Array(1, 2, 3, 4, 5); // new String(1)
```

There's one more special case to worry about. If you call the Array constructor with a single numeric argument, it does something completely different: It attempts to create an array with no elements but whose length property is the given argument. This means that ["hello"] and new Array("hello") behave the same, but [17] and new Array(17) do completely different things!

These are not necessarily difficult rules to learn, but it's clearer and less prone to accidental bugs to use array literals, which have more regular, consistent semantics.

Things to Remember

✦ The Array constructor behaves differently if its only argument is a number.

✦ Use array literals instead of the Array constructor.

Library and API Design

Every programmer is an API designer at one time or another. Maybe you don't have any immediate plans to write the next popular JavaScript library. But when you program in a platform for a long enough period of time, you build up a repertoire of solutions to common problems, and sooner or later you start to develop reusable utilities and components. Even if you don't release these as independent libraries, developing your skills as a library writer can help you write better components.

Designing libraries is a tricky business and is as much art as science. It's also incredibly important. APIs are a programmer's basic vocabulary. A well-designed API enables your users (which probably includes yourself!) to express their programs clearly, concisely, and unambiguously.

Item 53: Maintain Consistent Conventions

There are few decisions that affect API consumers more pervasively than the conventions you use for names and function signatures. These conventions have enormous influence: They establish the basic vocabulary and idioms of the applications that use them. Users of your library have to learn to read and write using these idioms, and it's your job to make that learning process as easy as possible. Inconsistency makes it harder to remember which conventions apply in which situations, which leads to more time spent consulting your library's documentation and less time spent getting real work done.

One of the key conventions is argument order. User interface libraries, for instance, usually have functions that accept multiple measurements such as width and height. Do your users a favor and make sure these always come in the same order. And it's worth choosing an order that matches other libraries—nearly all libraries accept width first, then height:

```
var widget = new Widget(320, 240); // width: 320, height: 240
```

Unless you have a really strong reason for needing to vary from universal practice, stick with what's familiar. If your library is meant for the web, remember that web developers routinely deal with multiple languages (HTML, CSS, and JavaScript... *at a minimum*). Don't make their lives even harder by needlessly varying from conventions they are likely to use in their normal workflow. For example, whenever CSS accepts parameters describing the four sides of a rectangle, it requires them in clockwise order starting from the top (top, right, bottom, left). So when writing a library with an analogous API, stick to this order. Your users will thank you. Or maybe they won't even notice—so much the better! But you can be sure they *will* notice if you deviate from standard convention.

If your API uses options objects (see Item 55), you can avoid the dependence on argument order. For standard options such as width/height measurements, you should pick a naming convention and adhere to it religiously. If one of your function signatures looks for width and height options and another looks for w and h, your users are in for a lifetime of constantly checking your documentation to remember which is used where. Similarly, if your Widget class has methods for setting properties, make sure you use the same naming convention for these update methods. There's no good reason for one class to have a setWidth method and another class to do the same thing with a method called width.

Every good library needs thorough documentation, but a great library treats its documentation as training wheels. Once your users get accustomed to your library's conventions, they should be able to do common tasks without ever checking the documentation. Consistent conventions can even help users guess what properties or methods are available without looking them up at all, or discover them at the console and guess their behavior from the names.

Things to Remember

+ Use consistent conventions for variable names and function signatures.

+ Don't deviate from conventions your users are likely to encounter in other parts of their development platform.

Item 54: Treat undefined As "No Value"

The undefined value is special: Whenever JavaScript has no specific value to provide it just produces undefined. Unassigned variables start out with the value undefined:

```
var x;
x; // undefined
```

Accessing nonexistent properties from objects produces undefined:

```
var obj = {};
obj.x; // undefined
```

Returning without a value or falling off the end of a function body produces the return value undefined:

```
function f() {
    return;
}

function g() { }

f(); // undefined
g(); // undefined
```

Function parameters that are not provided with actual arguments have the value undefined:

```
function f(x) {
    return x;
}

f(); // undefined
```

In each of these situations, the undefined value indicates that the operation did not result in a specific value. Of course, there's something a little paradoxical about a value that means "no value." But every operation has to produce *something*, so JavaScript uses undefined to fill the void (so to speak).

Treating undefined as the absence of any specific value is a convention established by the language. Using it for other purposes is a risky proposition. For example, a library of user interface elements might support a highlight method for changing the background color of an element:

```
element.highlight();          // use the default color
element.highlight("yellow");  // use a custom color
```

What if we wanted to provide a way to request a random color? We could use undefined as a special value for that purpose:

```
element.highlight(undefined); // use a random color
```

But this would be at odds with undefined's usual meaning. This makes it easy to get the wrong behavior when getting the value from another source, particularly one that might not have a value to provide. For example, a program might be using a configuration object with an optional color preference:

```
var config = JSON.parse(preferences);
// ...
element.highlight(config.highlightColor); // may be random
```

If the preferences do not specify a color, the programmer will most likely expect to get the default, just as if no value were provided. But by repurposing undefined, we actually caused this code to generate a random color. A better API might use a special color name for the random case:

```
element.highlight("random");
```

Sometimes it's not possible for an API to choose a special string value that's distinguishable from the normal set of string values accepted by the function. In these cases, there are special values other than undefined, such as null or true. But these tend not to lead to very readable code:

```
element.highlight(null);
```

For someone who is reading the code and may not have your library committed to memory, this code is rather opaque. In fact, a first guess might be that it removes highlighting. A more explicit and descriptive option is to represent the random case as an object with a random property (see Item 55 for more on options objects):

```
element.highlight({ random: true });
```

Another place to watch out for undefined is in the implementation of optional arguments. In theory, the arguments object (see Item 51) makes it possible to detect whether an argument was passed, but in practice, testing for undefined leads to more robust APIs. For example, a web server might take an optional host name:

```
var s1 = new Server(80, "example.com");
var s2 = new Server(80); // defaults to "localhost"
```

The Server constructor could be implemented by testing arguments.length:

```
function Server(port, hostname) {
    if (arguments.length < 2) {
        hostname = "localhost";
    }
```

```
        hostname = String(hostname);
        // ...
}
```

But this has a similar problem to the element.highlight method above. If a program provides an explicit argument by requesting a value from another source such as a configuration object, it might produce undefined:

```
var s3 = new Server(80, config.hostname);
```

If there's no hostname preference specified by config, the natural behavior is to use the default "localhost". But the above implementation ends up with the host name "undefined". It's better to test for undefined, which could be produced by leaving off the argument or by providing an argument expression that turns out to be undefined:

```
function Server(port, hostname) {
    if (hostname === undefined) {
        hostname = "localhost";
    }
    hostname = String(hostname);
    // ...
}
```

A reasonable alternative is to test whether hostname is truthy (see Item 3). Logical operators make this convenient:

```
function Server(port, hostname) {
    hostname = String(hostname || "localhost");
    // ...
}
```

This version uses the logical OR operator (||), which returns the first argument if it is a truthy value and otherwise returns its second argument. So, if hostname is undefined or an empty string, the expression (hostname || "localhost") evaluates to "localhost". As such, this is technically testing for more than undefined—it will treat all falsy values the same as undefined. This is probably acceptable for Server since an empty string is not a valid host name. So, if you are happy with a looser API that coerces all falsy values to a default value, truthiness testing is a concise way to implement parameter default values.

But beware: Truthiness is not always a safe test. If a function should accept the empty string as a legal value, a truthy test will override the empty string and replace it with the default value. Similarly, a function that accepts a number should not use a truthy test if it allows 0 (or NaN, although it's less common) as an acceptable value.

For example, a function for creating a user interface element might allow an element to have a width or height of 0, but provide a different default value:

```
var c1 = new Element(0, 0); // width: 0, height: 0
var c2 = new Element();     // width: 320, height: 240
```

An implementation that uses truthiness would be buggy:

```
function Element(width, height) {
    this.width = width || 320;   // wrong test
    this.height = height || 240; // wrong test
    // ...
}

var c1 = new Element(0, 0);

c1.width;  // 320
c1.height; // 240
```

Instead, we have to resort to the more verbose test for undefined:

```
function Element(width, height) {
    this.width = width === undefined ? 320 : width;
    this.height = height === undefined ? 240 : height;
    // ...
}

var c1 = new Element(0, 0);

c1.width;  // 0
c1.height; // 0

var c2 = new Element();

c2.width;  // 320
c2.height; // 240
```

Things to Remember

+ Avoid using undefined to represent anything other than the absence of a specific value.

+ Use descriptive string values or objects with named boolean properties, rather than undefined or null, to represent application-specific flags.

+ Test for undefined instead of checking arguments.length to provide parameter default values.

✦ Never use truthiness tests for parameter default values that should allow 0, NaN, or the empty string as valid arguments.

Item 55: Accept Options Objects for Keyword Arguments

Keeping consistent conventions for argument order, as Item 53 suggests, is important for helping programmers remember what each argument in a function call means. This works to a point. But it simply doesn't scale beyond a few arguments. Try making sense of a function call such as the following:

```
var alert = new Alert(100, 75, 300, 200,
                      "Error", message,
                      "blue", "white", "black",
                      "error", true);
```

We've all seen APIs like this. It's often the result of *argument creep*, where a function starts out simple, but over time, as the library expands in functionality, the signature acquires more and more arguments.

Fortunately, JavaScript provides a simple, lightweight idiom that works well for larger function signatures: the *options object*. An options object is a single argument that provides additional argument data through its named properties. The object literal form makes this especially pleasant to read and write:

```
var alert = new Alert({
    x: 100, y: 75,
    width: 300, height: 200,
    title: "Error", message: message,
    titleColor: "blue", bgColor: "white", textColor: "black",
    icon: "error", modal: true
});
```

This API is a little more verbose, but noticeably easier to read. Each argument becomes *self-documenting:* There's no need for a comment explaining its role, since its property name explains it perfectly. This is especially helpful for boolean parameters such as modal: Someone reading a call to new Alert might be able to infer the purpose of a string argument from its contents, but a naked true or false is not particularly informative.

Another benefit of options objects is that any of the arguments can be optional, and a caller can provide any subset of the optional arguments. With ordinary arguments (sometimes called *positional* arguments, since they are distinguished not by name but by their position in the argument list), optional arguments can often introduce ambiguities. For example, if we want both the position and the size of an Alert object to be optional, then it's not clear how to interpret a call such as this:

```
var alert = new Alert(app,
                      150, 150,
                      "Error", message,
                      "blue", "white", "black",
                      "error", true);
```

Are the first two numbers meant to specify the x and y or width and height arguments? With an options object, there's no question:

```
var alert = new Alert({
    parent: app,
    width: 150, height: 100,
    title: "Error", message: message,
    titleColor: "blue", bgColor: "white", textColor: "black",
    icon: "error", modal: true
});
```

Traditionally, options objects consist exclusively of optional arguments, so it's even possible to omit the object entirely:

```
var alert = new Alert(); // use all default parameter values
```

If there are one or two required arguments, it's better to keep them separate from the options object:

```
var alert = new Alert(app, message, {
    width: 150, height: 100,
    title: "Error",
    titleColor: "blue", bgColor: "white", textColor: "black",
    icon: "error", modal: true
});
```

Implementing a function that accepts an options object takes a little more work. Here is a thorough implementation:

```
function Alert(parent, message, opts) {
    opts = opts || {}; // default to an empty options object
    this.width = opts.width === undefined ? 320 : opts.width;
    this.height = opts.height === undefined
                  ? 240
                  : opts.height;
    this.x = opts.x === undefined
             ? (parent.width / 2) - (this.width / 2)
             : opts.x;
```

```
  this.y = opts.y === undefined
          ? (parent.height / 2) - (this.height / 2)
          : opts.y;
  this.title = opts.title || "Alert";
  this.titleColor = opts.titleColor || "gray";
  this.bgColor = opts.bgColor || "white";
  this.textColor = opts.textColor || "black";
  this.icon = opts.icon || "info";
  this.modal = !!opts.modal;
  this.message = message;
}
```

The implementation starts by providing a default empty options object, using the || operator (see Item 54). The numeric arguments test for undefined as Item 54 advises, since 0 is a valid value but not the default. For the string parameters, we use logical OR under the assumption that an empty string is not a valid value and should be replaced by a default value. The modal parameter coerces its argument to a boolean with a double negation pattern (!!).

This code is a little more verbose than it would be with positional arguments. Now, it's worth paying the price within the library if it makes users' lives easier. But we can make our own life easier with a useful abstraction: an object *extension* or *merging* function. Many JavaScript libraries and frameworks come with an extend function, which takes a *target* object and a *source* object and copies the properties of the latter object into the former. One of the most useful applications of this utility is for abstracting out the logic of merging default values and user-provided values for options objects. With the help of extend, the Alert function looks quite a bit cleaner:

```
function Alert(parent, message, opts) {
    opts = extend({
        width: 320,
        height: 240
    }, opts);
    opts = extend({
        x: (parent.width / 2) - (opts.width / 2),
        y: (parent.height / 2) - (opts.height / 2),
        title: "Alert",
        titleColor: "gray",
        bgColor: "white",
        textColor: "black",
        icon: "info",
        modal: false
    }, opts);
```

```
    this.width = opts.width;
    this.height = opts.height;
    this.x = opts.x;
    this.y = opts.y;
    this.title = opts.title;
    this.titleColor = opts.titleColor;
    this.bgColor = opts.bgColor;
    this.textColor = opts.textColor;
    this.icon = opts.icon;
    this.modal = opts.modal;
}
```

This avoids constantly reimplementing the logic of checking for the presence of each argument. Notice how we use two calls to extend, since the default values for x and y depend on first computing the values of width and height.

We can clean this up even further if all we want to do with the options is copy them into this:

```
function Alert(parent, message, opts) {
    opts = extend({
        width: 320,
        height: 240
    }, opts);
    opts = extend({
        x: (parent.width / 2) - (opts.width / 2),
        y: (parent.height / 2) - (opts.height / 2),
        title: "Alert",
        titleColor: "gray",
        bgColor: "white",
        textColor: "black",
        icon: "info",
        modal: false
    }, opts);
    extend(this, opts);
}
```

Different frameworks provide different variations of extend, but typically the implementation works by enumerating the properties of the source object and copying them into the target whenever they are not undefined:

```
function extend(target, source) {
    if (source) {
        for (var key in source) {
            var val = source[key];
```

```
            if (typeof val !== "undefined") {
                target[key] = val;
            }
        }
    }
    return target;
}
```

Notice that there are small differences between the original version of Alert and the implementation using extend. For one, our conditional logic in the first version avoids even computing the default values if they aren't needed. As long as computing the defaults has no side effects such as modifying the user interface or sending a network request—which is usually the case—this isn't really a problem. Another difference is in the logic for determining whether a value was provided. In our first version, we treat an empty string the same as undefined for the various string arguments. But it's more consistent to treat only undefined as a missing argument; using the || operator was more expedient but a less uniform policy for providing default parameter values. Uniformity is a good goal in library design, because it leads to better predictability for consumers of the API.

Things to Remember

✦ Use options objects to make APIs more readable and memorable.

✦ The arguments provided by an options object should all be treated as optional.

✦ Use an extend utility function to abstract out the logic of extracting values from options objects.

Item 56: Avoid Unnecessary State

APIs are sometimes classified as either *stateful* or *stateless*. A stateless API provides functions or methods whose behavior depends only on their inputs, not on the changing state of the program. The methods of a string are stateless: The string's contents cannot be modified, and the methods depend only on the contents of the string and the arguments passed to the method. No matter what else is going on in a program, the expression "foo".toUpperCase() will always produce "FOO". The methods of a Date object, by contrast, are stateful: Calling toString on the same Date object can produce different results based on whether the Date's properties have been modified by its various set methods.

While state is sometimes essential, stateless APIs tend to be easier to learn and use, more self-documenting, and less error-prone. A famous stateful API is the web's `Canvas` library, which provides user interface elements with methods for drawing shapes and images onto their surface. A program can draw text onto a canvas using the `fillText` method:

```
c.fillText("hello, world!", 75, 25);
```

This method provides a string to draw and a position in the canvas. But it doesn't specify other attributes of the drawn text such as its color, transparency, or text style. All of these attributes are specified separately by changing the internal state of the canvas:

```
c.fillStyle = "blue";
c.font = "24pt serif";
c.textAlign = "center";
c.fillText("hello, world!", 75, 25);
```

A less stateful version of the API might instead look like this:

```
c.fillText("hello, world!", 75, 25, {
    fillStyle: "blue",
    font: "24pt serif",
    textAlign: "center"
});
```

Why might the latter be preferable? First of all, it's much less fragile. The stateful API requires modifying the internal state of a canvas in order to do anything custom, and this causes one drawing operation to affect another one, even if they have nothing to do with each other. For example, the default fill style is black. But you can only count on getting the default value if you know that no one has changed the defaults already. If you want to do a drawing operation that uses the default color after changing it, you have to specify the default explicitly:

```
c.fillText("text 1", 0, 0); // default color
c.fillStyle = "blue";
c.fillText("text 2", 0, 30); // blue
c.fillStyle = "black";
c.fillText("text 3", 0, 60); // back in black
```

Compare this to a stateless API, which would automatically enable the reuse of default values:

```
c.fillText("text 1", 0, 0); // default color
c.fillText("text 2", 0, 30, { fillStyle: "blue" }); // blue
c.fillText("text 3", 0, 60); // default color
```

Notice also how each statement becomes more readable: To understand what any individual call to fillText does, you don't have to understand all the modifications that precede it. In fact, the canvas might even be modified in some completely separate part of the program. This can easily lead to bugs, where one piece of code written somewhere else changes the state of the canvas:

```
c.fillStyle = "blue";
drawMyImage(c); // did drawMyImage change c?
c.fillText("hello, world!", 75, 25);
```

To understand what happens in the last line, we have to know what modifications drawMyImage might make to the canvas. A stateless API leads to more modular code, which avoids bugs based on surprising interactions between different parts of your code, while simultaneously making the code easier to read.

Stateful APIs are also more difficult to learn. Reading the documentation for fillText, you can't tell what aspects of the state of a canvas affect the drawing. Even if some of them are easy to guess, it's hard for a nonexpert to know whether they've correctly initialized all of the necessary state. It's of course possible to provide an exhaustive list in the documentation of fillText. And when you do need a stateful API, you should definitely document the state dependencies carefully. But a stateless API eliminates these implicit dependencies altogether, so they don't need the extra documentation in the first place.

Another benefit of stateless APIs is conciseness. A stateful API tends to lead to a proliferation of additional statements just to set the internal state of an object before calling its methods. Consider a parser for the popular "INI" configuration file format. For example, a simple INI file might look like this:

```
[Host]
address=172.0.0.1
name=localhost
[Connections]
timeout=10000
```

One approach to an API for this kind of data would be to provide a setSection method for selecting a section before looking up configuration parameters with a get method:

```
var ini = INI.parse(src);

ini.setSection("Host");
var addr = ini.get("address");
var hostname = ini.get("name");
```

```
ini.setSection("Connection");
var timeout = ini.get("timeout");
var server = new Server(addr, hostname, timeout);
```

But with a stateless API, it's not necessary to create extra variables like addr and hostname to save the extracted data before updating the section:

```
var ini = INI.parse(src);
var server = new Server(ini.Host.address,
                        ini.Host.name,
                        ini.Connection.timeout);
```

Notice how once we make the section explicit we can simply represent the ini object as a dictionary, and each section as a dictionary, making the API even simpler. (See Chapter 5 to learn more about dictionary objects.)

Things to Remember

+ Prefer stateless APIs where possible.

+ When providing stateful APIs, document the relevant state that each operation depends on.

Item 57: Use Structural Typing for Flexible Interfaces

Imagine a library for creating *wikis:* web sites containing content that users can interactively create, delete, and modify. Many wikis feature simple, text-based markup languages for creating content. These markup languages typically provide a subset of the available features of HTML, but with a simpler and more legible source format. For example, text might be formatted by surrounding it with asterisks for bold, underscores for underlining, and forward slashes for italics. Users can enter text such as this:

```
This sentence contains a *bold phrase* within it.
This sentence contains an _underlined phrase_ within it.
This sentence contains an /italicized phrase/ within it.
```

The site would then display the content to wiki readers as:

This sentence contains a **bold phrase** within it.

This sentence contains an <u>underlined phrase</u> within it.

This sentence contains an *italicized phrase* within it.

A flexible wiki library might provide application writers with a choice of markup languages, since many different popular formats have emerged over the years.

To make this work, we need to separate the functionality of extracting the contents of user-created markup source text from the rest of the wiki functionality, such as account management, revision history, and content storage. The rest of the application should interact with the extraction functionality through an *interface* with a well-documented set of properties and methods. By programming strictly to the interface's documented API and ignoring the implementation details of those methods, the rest of the application can function correctly regardless of which source format an application chooses to use.

Let's look a little more closely at what kind of interface is needed for wiki content extraction. The library must be able to extract metadata such as page title and author and to format page contents as HTML for displaying to wiki readers. We can represent each page in the wiki as an object that provides access to this data through page methods such as getTitle, getAuthor, and toHTML.

Next, the library needs to provide a way to create an application with a custom wiki formatter, as well as some built-in formatters for popular markup formats. For example, an application writer might wish to use the MediaWiki format (the format used by Wikipedia):

```
var app = new Wiki(Wiki.formats.MEDIAWIKI);
```

The library would store this formatter function internally in the Wiki instance object:

```
function Wiki(format) {
    this.format = format;
}
```

Whenever a reader wants to view a page, the application retrieves its source and renders an HTML page using the internal formatter:

```
Wiki.prototype.displayPage = function(source) {
    var page = this.format(source);
    var title = page.getTitle();
    var author = page.getAuthor();
    var output = page.toHTML();
    // ...
};
```

How would a formatter such as Wiki.formats.MEDIAWIKI be implemented? Programmers familiar with class-based programming might be inclined to create a base Page class that represents the user-created content and implement each different format as a subclass of Page. The MediaWiki format would be implemented with a class MWPage that extends Page, and MEDIAWIKI would be a "factory function" that returns an instance of MWPage:

```
function MWPage(source) {
    Page.call(this, source); // call the super-constructor
    // ...
}

// MWPage extends Page
MWPage.prototype = Object.create(Page.prototype);

MWPage.prototype.getTitle = /* ... */;
MWPage.prototype.getAuthor = /* ... */;
MWPage.prototype.toHTML = /* ... */;

Wiki.formats.MEDIAWIKI = function(source) {
    return new MWPage(source);
};
```

(See Chapter 4 for more about implementing class hierarchies with constructors and prototypes.) But what practical purpose does the base Page class serve? Since MWPage needs its own implementation of the methods required by the wiki application—getTitle, getAuthor, and toHTML—there's not necessarily any useful implementation code to inherit. Notice, too, that the displayPage method above does not care about the inheritance hierarchy of the page object; it only requires the relevant methods in order to work. So implementations of wiki formats are free to implement those methods however they like.

Where many object-oriented languages encourage structuring your programs around classes and inheritance, JavaScript tends not to stand on ceremony. It is often perfectly sufficient to provide an implementation for an interface like the MediaWiki page format with a simple object literal:

```
Wiki.formats.MEDIAWIKI = function(source) {
    // extract contents from source
    // ...
    return {
        getTitle: function() { /* ... */ },
        getAuthor: function() { /* ... */ },
        toHTML: function() { /* ... */ }
    };
};
```

What's more, inheritance sometimes causes more problems than it solves. This becomes evident when several different wiki formats share nonoverlapping sets of functionality: There may not be any inheritance hierarchy that makes sense. For example, imagine three formats:

Format A: *bold*, [Link], /italics/

Format B: **bold**, [[Link]], *italics*

Format C: **bold**, [Link], *italics*

We would like to implement individual pieces of functionality for recognizing each different kind of input, but the mixing and matching of functionality just doesn't map to any clear hierarchical relationship between A, B, and C (I welcome you to try it!). The right thing to do is to implement separate functions for each kind of input matching—single asterisks, double asterisks, slashes, brackets, and so on—and mix and match functionality as needed for each format.

Notice that by eliminating the Page superclass, we don't have to replace it with anything. This is where JavaScript's dynamic typing really shines. Anyone who wishes to implement a new custom format can do so without needing to "register" it somewhere. The displayPage method works with any JavaScript object whatsoever, so long as it has the proper structure: the expected getTitle, getAuthor, and getHTML methods, each with the expected behavior.

This kind of interface is sometimes known as *structural typing* or *duck typing:* Any object will do so long as it has the expected structure (if it looks like a duck, swims like a duck, and quacks like a duck...). It's an elegant programming pattern and especially lightweight in dynamic languages such as JavaScript, since it doesn't require you to write anything explicit. A function that calls methods on an object will work on any object that implements the same interface. Of course, you should list out the expectations of an object interface in your API documentation. This way, implementers know what properties and methods are required, and what your libraries or applications expect of their behavior.

Another benefit of the flexibility of structural typing is for unit testing. Our wiki library probably expects to be plugged into an HTTP server object that implements the networking functionality of the wiki. If we want to test the interaction sequences of the wiki without actually connecting to the network, we can implement a *mock object* that pretends to behave like a live HTTP server but follows a prescribed script instead of touching the network. This provides a repeatable interaction with a fake server, instead of relying on the unpredictable behavior of the network, making it possible to test the behavior of components that interact with the server.

Things to Remember

✦ Use structural typing (also known as duck typing) for flexible object interfaces.

✦ Avoid inheritance when structural interfaces are more flexible and lightweight.

✦ Use mock objects, that is, alternative implementations of interfaces that provide repeatable behavior, for unit testing.

Item 58: Distinguish between Array and Array-Like

Consider two different class APIs. The first is for *bit vectors:* ordered collections of bits.

```
var bits = new BitVector();

bits.enable(4);
bits.enable([1, 3, 8, 17]);

bits.bitAt(4); // 1
bits.bitAt(8); // 1
bits.bitAt(9); // 0
```

Notice that the enable method is *overloaded:* You can pass it either an index or an array of indices.

The second class API is for *string sets:* unordered collections of strings.

```
var set = new StringSet();

set.add("Hamlet");
set.add(["Rosencrantz", "Guildenstern"]);
set.add({ "Ophelia": 1, "Polonius": 1, "Horatio": 1 });

set.contains("Polonius");      // true
set.contains("Guildenstern"); // true
set.contains("Falstaff");      // false
```

Similar to the enable method of bit vectors, the add method is also overloaded, but in addition to strings and arrays of strings, it also accepts a dictionary object.

To implement `BitVector.prototype.enable`, we can avoid the question of how to determine whether an object is an array by testing the other case first:

```
BitVector.prototype.enable = function(x) {
    if (typeof x === "number") {
        this.enableBit(x);
    } else { // assume x is array-like
        for (var i = 0, n = x.length; i < n; i++) {
            this.enableBit(x[i]);
        }
    }
};
```

No problem. What about `StringSet.prototype.add`? Now we seem to need to distinguish between arrays and objects. But that question doesn't even make sense—JavaScript arrays *are* objects! What we really want to do is separate out array objects from nonarray objects.

Making this distinction is at odds with JavaScript's flexible notion of "array-like" objects (see Item 51). Any object can be treated as an array as long as it obeys the right interface. And there's no clear way to test an object to see whether it's intended to satisfy an interface. We might try to guess that an object that has a `length` property is intended to be an array, but this is no guarantee; what if we happen to use a dictionary object that has the key `"length"` in it?

```
dimensions.add({
    "length": 1, // implies array-like?
    "height": 1,
    "width":  1
});
```

Using imprecise heuristics to determine their interface is a recipe for misunderstanding and misuse. Guessing whether an object implements a structural type is sometimes known as *duck testing* (after the "duck types" described in Item 57), and it's bad practice. Since objects are not tagged with explicit information to indicate the structural types they implement, there's no reliable, programmatic way to detect this information.

Overloading two types means there must be a way to distinguish the cases. And it's not possible to detect that a value implements a structural interface. This leads to the following rule:

APIs should never overload structural types with other overlapping types.

For StringSet, the answer is not to use the structural "array-like" interface in the first place. We should instead choose a type that carries a well-defined "tag" indicating that the user truly intends it to be an array. An obvious but imperfect choice is to use the instanceof operator to test whether an object inherits from Array.prototype:

```
StringSet.prototype.add = function(x) {
    if (typeof x === "string") {
        this.addString(x);
    } else if (x instanceof Array) { // too restrictive
        x.forEach(function(s) {
            this.addString(s);
        }, this);
    } else {
        for (var key in x) {
            this.addString(key);
        }
    }
};
```

After all, we know for sure that anytime an object is an instance of Array, it behaves like an array. But this time it turns out that this is too *fine* a distinction. In environments where there can be multiple global objects, there may be multiple copies of the standard Array constructor and prototype object. This happens in the browser, where each frame gets a separate copy of the standard library. When communicating values between frames, an array from one frame will not inherit from the Array.prototype of another frame.

For this reason, ES5 introduced the Array.isArray function, which tests whether a value is an array, regardless of prototype inheritance. In ECMAScript standards-ese, this function tests whether the value of the internal [[Class]] property of the object is "Array". When you need to test whether an object is a true array, not just an array-like object, Array.isArray is more reliable than instanceof.

This leads to a more robust implementation of the add method:

```
StringSet.prototype.add = function(x) {
    if (typeof x === "string") {
        this.addString(x);
    } else if (Array.isArray(x)) { // tests for true arrays
        x.forEach(function(s) {
            this.addString(s);
        }, this);
    } else {
```

```
        for (var key in x) {
            this.addString(key);
        }
    }
};
```

In environments that don't support ES5, you can use the standard `Object.prototype.toString` method to test whether an object is an array:

```
var toString = Object.prototype.toString;

function isArray(x) {
    return toString.call(x) === "[object Array]";
}
```

The `Object.prototype.toString` function uses the internal [[Class]] property of an object to create its result string, so it too is a more reliable method than `instanceof` for testing whether an object is an array.

Notice that this version of add has different behavior that affects consumers of the API. The array version of the overloaded API does not accept arbitrary array-like objects. You can't, for example, pass an arguments object and expect it to be treated as an array:

```
function MyClass() {
    this.keys = new StringSet();
    // ...
}

MyClass.prototype.update = function() {
    this.keys.add(arguments); // treated as a dictionary
};
```

Instead, the correct way to use add is to convert the object to a true array, using the idiom described in Item 51:

```
MyClass.prototype.update = function() {
    this.keys.add([].slice.call(arguments));
};
```

Callers need to do this conversion whenever they want to pass an array-like object to an API that expects a true array. For this reason, it's necessary to document which of the two types your API accepts. In the examples above, the enable method accepts numbers and array-like objects, whereas the add method accepts strings, true arrays, and (nonarray) objects.

Things to Remember

+ Never overload structural types with other overlapping types.

+ When overloading a structural type with other types, test for the other types first.

+ Accept true arrays instead of array-like objects when overloading with other object types.

+ Document whether your API accepts true arrays or array-like values.

+ Use ES5's `Array.isArray` to test for true arrays.

Item 59: Avoid Excessive Coercion

JavaScript is notoriously lax about types (see Item 3). Many of the standard operators and libraries automatically coerce their arguments to the expected type rather than throwing exceptions for unexpected inputs. Without additional logic, building off of these built-in operations inherits their coercing behavior:

```
function square(x) {
    return x * x;
}
```

```
square("3"); // 9
```

Coercions can certainly be convenient. But as Item 3 points out, they can also cause trouble, hiding errors and leading to erratic and hard-to-diagnose behavior.

Coercions are especially confusing when working with overloaded function signatures, like the `enable` method of the bit vector class of Item 58. The method uses its argument's type to determine its behavior. The signature would become harder to understand if `enable` attempted to coerce its argument to an expected type. Which type should it choose? Coercing to a number completely breaks the overloading:

```
BitVector.prototype.enable = function(x) {
    x = Number(x);
    if (typeof x === "number") { // always true
        this.enableBit(x);
    } else {                     // never executed
        for (var i = 0, n = x.length; i < n; i++) {
            this.enableBit(x[i]);
        }
    }
};
```

As a general rule, it's wise to avoid coercing arguments whose type is used to determine an overloaded function's behavior. Coercions make it harder to tell which variant you will end up with. Imagine trying to make sense of this use:

```
bits.enable("100"); // number or array-like?
```

This use of enable is ambiguous: The caller could plausibly have intended the argument to be treated as a number or as an array of bit values. But our constructor was not designed for strings, so there's no way to know. It's likely an indication that the caller didn't understand the API. In fact, if we wanted to be a little more careful in our API, we could enforce that only numbers and objects are accepted:

```
BitVector.prototype.enable = function(x) {
    if (typeof x === "number") {
        this.enableBit(x);
    } else if (typeof x === "object" && x) {
        for (var i = 0, n = x.length; i < n; i++) {
            this.enableBit(x[i]);
        }
    } else {
        throw new TypeError("expected number or array-like");
    }
}
```

This last version of enable is an example of a more cautious style known as *defensive programming,* which attempts to defend against potential errors with additional checks. In general, it's not possible to defend against all possible bugs. For example, we could also check to ensure that if x is an object it also has a length property, but this wouldn't protect against, say, an accidental use of a String object. And JavaScript provides only very rudimentary tools for implementing these checks, such as the typeof operator, but it's possible to write utility functions to guard function signatures more concisely. For example, we could guard the BitVector constructor with a single up-front check:

```
function BitVector(x) {
    uint32.or(arrayLike).guard(x);
    // ...
}
```

To make this work, we can build a utility library of guard objects with the help of a shared prototype object that implements the guard method:

```
var guard = {
    guard: function(x) {
        if (!this.test(x)) {
```

```
            throw new TypeError("expected " + this);
        }
    }
};
```

Each guard object then implements its own test method and string description for error messages:

```
var uint32 = Object.create(guard);

uint32.test = function(x) {
    return typeof x === "number" && x === (x >>> 0);
};

uint32.toString = function() {
    return "uint32";
};
```

The uint32 guard uses a trick of JavaScript's bitwise operators to perform a conversion to an unsigned 32-bit integer. The *unsigned right shift operator* converts its first argument to an unsigned 32-bit integer before performing a bitwise shift (see Item 2). Shifting by zero bits then has no effect on the integer value. So uint32.test effectively compares a number to the result of converting it to an unsigned 32-bit integer.

Next we can implement the arrayLike guard object:

```
var arrayLike = Object.create(guard);

arrayLike.test = function(x) {
    return typeof x === "object" && x && uint32.test(x.length);
};

arrayLike.toString = function() {
    return "array-like object";
};
```

Notice that we have taken defensive programming one step further here, ensuring that an array-like object should have an unsigned integer length property.

Lastly, we can implement "chaining" methods (see Item 60), such as or, as prototype methods:

```
guard.or = function(other) {
    var result = Object.create(guard);
```

```
    var self = this;
    result.test = function(x) {
        return self.test(x) || other.test(x);
    };

    var description = this + " or " + other;
    result.toString = function() {
        return description;
    };

    return result;
};
```

This method combines the receiver guard object (the object bound to this) with a second guard object (the other parameter), producing a new guard object whose test and toString methods combine the two input objects' methods. Notice that we use a local self variable to save a reference to this (see Items 25 and 37) for use inside the resultant guard object's test method.

These tests can help catch bugs earlier when they crop up, which makes them significantly easier to diagnose. Nevertheless, they can clutter a codebase and potentially affect application performance. Whether to use defensive programming is a question of cost (the number of extra tests you have to write and execute) versus benefit (the number of bugs you catch earlier, saving development and debugging time).

Things to Remember

✦ Avoid mixing coercions with overloading.

✦ Consider defensively guarding against unexpected inputs.

Item 60: Support Method Chaining

Part of the power of stateless APIs (see Item 56) is their flexibility for building compound operations out of smaller ones. A great example is the replace method of strings. Since the result is itself a string, we can perform multiple replacements by repeatedly calling replace on the result of the previous method call. A common usage of this pattern is for replacing special characters of a string before inserting it into HTML:

```
function escapeBasicHTML(str) {
    return str.replace(/&/g, "&amp;")
            .replace(/</g, "&lt;")
```

```
        .replace(/>/g, "&gt;")
        .replace(/"/g, "&quot;")
        .replace(/'/g, "&apos;");
}
```

The first call to `replace` returns a string with all instances of the special character `"&"` replaced with the HTML escape sequence `"&amp;"`; the second call then replaces any instances of `"<"` with the escape sequence `"&lt;"`, and so on. This style of repeated method calls is known as *method chaining*. It's not necessary to write in this style, but it's much more concise than saving each intermediate result to an intermediate variable:

```
function escapeBasicHTML(str1) {
    var str2 = str1.replace(/&/g, "&amp;");
    var str3 = str2.replace(/</g, "&lt;");
    var str4 = str3.replace(/>/g, "&gt;");
    var str5 = str4.replace(/"/g, "&quot;");
    var str6 = str5.replace(/'/g, "&apos;");
    return str6;
}
```

Eliminating the temporary variables makes it clearer to readers of the code that the intermediate results are only important as a step along the way to the final result.

Method chaining can be used whenever an API produces objects of some interface (see Item 57) with methods that produce more objects, often of the same interface. The array iteration methods described in Items 50 and 51 are another great example of a "chainable" API:

```
var users = records.map(function(record) {
                  return record.username;
              })
              .filter(function(username) {
                  return !!username;
              })
              .map(function(username) {
                  return username.toLowerCase();
              });
```

This chained operation takes an array of objects representing user records, extracts the username property of each record, filters out any empty usernames, and finally converts the usernames to lowercase strings.

This style is so flexible and expressive for consumers of an API, that it's worth designing your API to support it. Often, in stateless APIs, "chainability" falls out as a natural consequence: If your API does not modify an object it has to return a new object. As a result, you get an API whose methods all produce more objects with similar sets of methods.

Method chaining is also useful to support in a stateful setting. The trick here is for methods that update an object to return this instead of undefined. This makes it possible to perform multiple updates on the same object via a sequence of chained method calls:

```
element.setBackgroundColor("yellow")
       .setColor("red")
       .setFontWeight("bold");
```

Method chaining for stateful APIs is sometimes known as the *fluent style*. (The term was coined by programmers simulating Smalltalk's "method cascades"; a built-in syntax for calling multiple methods on a single object.) If the update methods do not return this, then the user of the API has to repeat the name of the object each time. If the object is simply named by a variable, this doesn't make much difference. But when combining stateless methods that retrieve objects with update methods, method chaining can make for very concise and readable code. The front-end library jQuery popularized this approach with a set of (stateless) methods for "querying" a web page for user interface elements and a set of (stateful) methods for updating those elements:

```
$("#notification")                        // find notification element
    .html("Server not responding.") // set notification message
    .removeClass("info")                  // remove one set of styling
    .addClass("error");                   // add more styling
```

Since the stateful calls to the html, removeClass, and addClass methods support the fluent style by returning the same object, we don't even have to create a temporary variable for the result of the query performed by the jQuery function ($). Of course, if users find this style too terse, they can always introduce a variable to name the result of the query:

```
var element = $("#notification");
element.html("Server not responding.");
element.removeClass("info");
element.addClass("error");
```

But by supporting method chaining, the API allows programmers to decide for themselves which style they prefer. If the methods returned undefined, users would be forced to write in the more verbose style.

Things to Remember

✦ Use method chaining to combine stateless operations.

✦ Support method chaining by designing stateless methods that produce new objects.

✦ Support method chaining in stateful methods by returning `this`.

Concurrency

JavaScript was designed as an *embedded scripting language*. Java-Script programs do not run as stand-alone applications, but as scripts in the context of a larger application. The flagship example is, of course, the web browser. A browser can have many windows and tabs running multiple web applications, each responding to various inputs and stimuli: user actions via keyboard, mouse, or touch, the arrival of data from the network, or timed alarms. These events can occur at any point—even simultaneously—during the lifetime of a web application. And for each kind of event, the application may wish to be notified of information and respond with custom behavior.

JavaScript's approach to writing programs that respond to multiple concurrent events is remarkably user-friendly and powerful, using a combination of a simple execution model, sometimes known as *event-queue* or *event-loop concurrency*, with what are known as *asynchronous* APIs. Thanks to the effectiveness of this approach, as well as the fact that JavaScript is standardized independently of web browsers, JavaScript is used as the programming language for a variety of other applications, from desktop applications to server-side frameworks such as Node.js.

Curiously, the ECMAScript standard has, to date, never said a word about concurrency. Consequently, this chapter deals with "de facto" characteristics of JavaScript rather than the official standard. Nevertheless, most JavaScript environments share the same approach to concurrency, and future versions of the standard may standardize on this widely implemented execution model. Regardless of the standard, working with events and asynchronous APIs is a fundamental part of programming in JavaScript.

Item 61: Don't Block the Event Queue on I/O

JavaScript programs are structured around *events:* inputs that may come in simultaneously from a variety of external sources, such as interactions from a user (clicking a mouse button, pressing a key, or touching a screen), incoming network data, or scheduled alarms. In some languages, it's customary to write code that waits for a particular input:

```
var text = downloadSync("http://example.com/file.txt");
console.log(text);
```

(The console.log API is a common utility in JavaScript platforms for printing out debugging information to a developer console.) Functions such as downloadSync are known as *synchronous,* or *blocking:* The program stops doing any work while it waits for its input—in this case, the result of downloading a file over the internet. Since the computer could be doing other useful work while it waits for the download to complete, such languages typically provide the programmer with a way to create multiple *threads:* subcomputations that are executed concurrently, allowing one portion of the program to stop and wait for ("block on") a slow input while another portion of the program can carry on usefully doing independent work.

In JavaScript, most I/O operations are provided through *asynchronous,* or *nonblocking* APIs. Instead of blocking a thread on a result, the programmer provides a callback (see Item 19) for the system to invoke once the input arrives:

```
downloadAsync("http://example.com/file.txt", function(text) {
    console.log(text);
});
```

Rather than blocking on the network, this API initiates the download process and then immediately returns after storing the callback in an internal registry. At some point later, when the download has completed, the system calls the registered callback, passing it the text of the downloaded file as its argument.

Now, the system does not just jump right in and call the callback the instant the download completes. JavaScript is sometimes described as providing a *run-to-completion* guarantee: Any user code that is currently running in a shared context, such as a single web page in a browser, or a single running instance of a web server, is allowed to finish executing before the next event handler is invoked. In effect, the system maintains an internal queue of events as they occur, and invokes any registered callbacks one at a time.

Figure 7.1 shows an illustration of example event queues in client-side and server-side applications. As events occur, they are added to the end of the application's event queue (at the top of the diagram). The JavaScript system executes the application with an internal *event loop*, which plucks events off of the bottom of the queue—that is, in the order in which they were received—and calls any registered JavaScript event handlers (callbacks like the one passed to downloadAsync above) one at a time, passing the event data as arguments to the handlers.

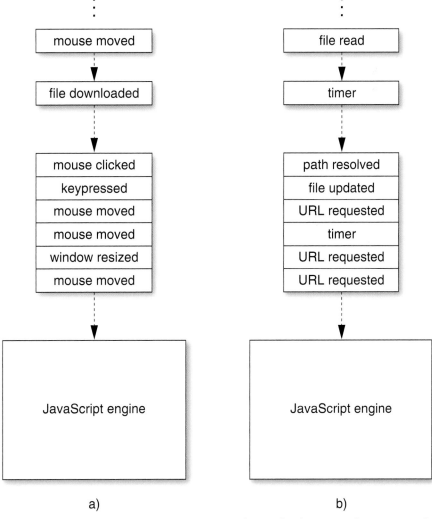

a)   b)

Figure 7.1 Example event queues in a) a web client application and b) a web server

The benefit of the run-to-completion guarantee is that when your code runs, you know that you have complete control over the application state: You never have to worry that some variable or object property will change out from under you due to concurrently executing code. This has the pleasant result that concurrent programming in Java-Script tends to be much easier than working with threads and locks in languages such as C++, Java, or C#.

Conversely, the drawback of run-to-completion is that any and all code you write effectively holds up the rest of the application from proceeding. In interactive applications like the browser, a blocked event handler prevents any other user input from being handled and can even prevent the rendering of a page, leading to an unresponsive user experience. In a server setting, a blocked handler can prevent other network requests from being handled, leading to an unresponsive server.

The single most important rule of concurrent JavaScript is never to use any blocking I/O APIs in the middle of an application's event queue. In the browser, hardly any blocking APIs are even available, although a few have sadly leaked into the platform over the years. The XMLHttpRequest library, which provides network I/O similar to the downloadAsync function above, has a synchronous version that is considered bad form. Synchronous I/O has disastrous consequences for the interactivity of a web application, preventing the user from interacting with a page until the I/O operation completes.

By contrast, asynchronous APIs are safe for use in an event-based setting, because they force your application logic to continue processing in a separate "turn" of the event loop. In the examples above, imagine that it takes a couple of seconds to download the URL. In that time, an enormous number of other events may occur. In the synchronous implementation, those events would pile up in the event queue, but the event loop would be stuck waiting for the JavaScript code to finish executing, preventing the processing of any other events. But in the asynchronous version, the JavaScript code registers an event handler and returns immediately, allowing other event handlers to process intervening events before the download completes.

In settings where the main application's event queue is unaffected, blocking operations are less problematic. For example, the web platform provides the Worker API, which makes it possible to spawn concurrent computations. Unlike conventional threads, workers are executed in a completely isolated state, with no access to the global scope or web page contents of the application's main thread, so they cannot interfere with the execution of code running in from the main event queue. In a worker, using the synchronous variant of XMLHttpRequest is less problematic; blocking on a download does prevent the Worker from continuing, but it does not prevent the page from rendering or the event queue from responding to events. In a server setting, blocking APIs are unproblematic during startup, that is, before the server begins responding to incoming requests. But when servicing requests, blocking APIs are every bit as catastrophic as in the event queue of the browser.

Things to Remember

✦ Asynchronous APIs take callbacks to defer processing of expensive operations and avoid blocking the main application.

✦ JavaScript accepts events concurrently but processes event handlers sequentially using an event queue.

✦ Never use blocking I/O in an application's event queue.

Item 62: Use Nested or Named Callbacks for Asynchronous Sequencing

Item 61 shows how asynchronous APIs perform potentially expensive I/O operations without blocking the application from continuing doing work and processing other input. Understanding the order of operations of asynchronous programs can be a little confusing at first. For example, this program prints out "starting" before it prints "finished", even though the two actions appear in the opposite order in the program source:

```
downloadAsync("file.txt", function(file) {
    console.log("finished");
});
console.log("starting");
```

The downloadAsync call returns immediately, without waiting for the file to finish downloading. Meanwhile, JavaScript's run-to-completion guarantee ensures that the next line executes before any other event handlers are executed. This means that "starting" is sure to print before "finished".

The easiest way to understand this sequence of operations is to think of an asynchronous API as *initiating* rather than *performing* an operation. The code above first initiates the download of a file and then immediately prints out "starting". When the download completes, in some separate turn of the event loop, the registered event handler prints "finished".

So, if placing several statements in a row only works if you need to do something after initiating an operation how do you sequence completed asynchronous operations? For example, what if we need to look up a URL in an asynchronous database and then download the contents of that URL? It's impossible to initiate both requests back-to-back:

```
db.lookupAsync("url", function(url) {
    // ?
});
downloadAsync(url, function(text) { // error: url is not bound
    console.log("contents of " + url + ": " + text);
});
```

This can't possibly work, because the URL resulting from the database lookup is needed as the argument to downloadAsync, but it's not in scope. And with good reason: All we've done at that step is initiate the database lookup; the result of the lookup simply isn't available yet.

The most straightforward answer is to use nesting. Thanks to the power of closures (see Item 11), we can embed the second action in the callback to the first:

```
db.lookupAsync("url", function(url) {
    downloadAsync(url, function(text) {
        console.log("contents of " + url + ": " + text);
    });
});
```

There are still two callbacks, but the second is contained within the first, creating a closure that has access to the outer callback's variables. Notice how the second callback refers to url.

Nesting asynchronous operations is easy, but it quickly gets unwieldy when scaling up to longer sequences:

```
db.lookupAsync("url", function(url) {
    downloadAsync(url, function(file) {
        downloadAsync("a.txt", function(a) {
            downloadAsync("b.txt", function(b) {
                downloadAsync("c.txt", function(c) {
                    // ...
                });
            });
        });
    });
});
```

One way to mitigate excessive nesting is to lift nested callbacks back out as named functions and pass them any additional data they need as extra arguments. The two-step example above could be rewritten as:

```
db.lookupAsync("url", downloadURL);

function downloadURL(url) {
    downloadAsync(url, function(text) { // still nested
        showContents(url, text);
    });
}

function showContents(url, text) {
    console.log("contents of " + url + ": " + text);
}
```

This still uses a nested callback inside downloadURL in order to combine the outer url variable with the inner text variable as arguments to showContents. We can eliminate this last nested callback with bind (see Item 25):

```
db.lookupAsync("url", downloadURL);

function downloadURL(url) {
    downloadAsync(url, showContents.bind(null, url));
}

function showContents(url, text) {
    console.log("contents of " + url + ": " + text);
}
```

This approach leads to more sequential-looking code, but at the cost of having to name each intermediate step of the sequence and copy bindings from step to step. This can get awkward in cases like the longer example above:

```
db.lookupAsync("url", downloadURLAndFiles);

function downloadURLAndFiles(url) {
    downloadAsync(url, downloadABC.bind(null, url));
}

// awkward name
function downloadABC(url, file) {
    downloadAsync("a.txt",
                    // duplicated bindings
                    downloadBC.bind(null, url, file));
}
```

```
// awkward name
function downloadBC(url, file, a) {
    downloadAsync("b.txt",
                  // more duplicated bindings
                  downloadC.bind(null, url, file, a));
}

// awkward name
function downloadC(url, file, a, b) {
    downloadAsync("c.txt",
                  // still more duplicated bindings
                  finish.bind(null, url, file, a, b));
}

function finish(url, file, a, b, c) {
    // ...
}
```

Sometimes a combination of the two approaches strikes a better balance, albeit still with some nesting:

```
db.lookupAsync("url", function(url) {
    downloadURLAndFiles(url);
});

function downloadURLAndFiles(url) {
    downloadAsync(url, downloadFiles.bind(null, url));
}

function downloadFiles(url, file) {
    downloadAsync("a.txt", function(a) {
        downloadAsync("b.txt", function(b) {
            downloadAsync("c.txt", function(c) {
                // ...
            });
        });
    });
}
```

Even better, this last step can be improved with an additional abstraction for downloading multiple files and storing them in an array:

```
function downloadFiles(url, file) {
    downloadAllAsync(["a.txt", "b.txt", "c.txt"],
                     function(all) {
```

```
        var a = all[0], b = all[1], c = all[2];
        // ...
    });
}
```

Using downloadAllAsync also allows us to download multiple files concurrently. Sequencing means that each operation cannot even be initiated until the previous one completes. And some operations are inherently sequential, like downloading the URL we fetched from a database lookup. But if we have a list of filenames to download, chances are there's no reason to wait for each file to finish downloading before requesting the next. Item 66 explains how to implement concurrent abstractions such as downloadAllAsync.

Beyond nesting and naming callbacks, it's possible to build higher-level abstractions to make asynchronous control flow simpler and more concise. Item 68 describes one particularly popular approach. Beyond that, it's worth exploring asynchrony libraries or experimenting with abstractions of your own.

Things to Remember

+ Use nested or named callbacks to perform several asynchronous operations in sequence.

+ Try to strike a balance between excessive nesting of callbacks and awkward naming of non-nested callbacks.

+ Avoid sequencing operations that can be performed concurrently.

Item 63: Be Aware of Dropped Errors

One of the more difficult aspects of asynchronous programming to manage is error handling. In synchronous code, it's easy to handle errors in one fell swoop by wrapping a section of code with a try block:

```
try {
    f();
    g();
    h();
} catch (e) {
    // handle any error that occurred...
}
```

With asynchronous code, a multistep process is usually divided into separate turns of the event queue, so it's not possible to wrap them all in a single try block. In fact, asynchronous APIs cannot even throw exceptions at all, because by the time an asynchronous error occurs, there is no obvious execution context to throw the exception to! Instead, asynchronous APIs tend to represent errors as special arguments to callbacks, or take additional error-handling callbacks (sometimes referred to as *errbacks*). For example, an asynchronous API for downloading a file like the one from Item 61 might take an extra function to be called in case of a network error:

```
downloadAsync("http://example.com/file.txt", function(text) {
    console.log("File contents: " + text);
}, function(error) {
    console.log("Error: " + error);
});
```

To download several files, you can nest the callbacks as explained in Item 62:

```
downloadAsync("a.txt", function(a) {
    downloadAsync("b.txt", function(b) {
        downloadAsync("c.txt", function(c) {
            console.log("Contents: " + a + b + c);
        }, function(error) {
            console.log("Error: " + error);
        });
    }, function(error) { // repeated error-handling logic
        console.log("Error: " + error);
    });
}, function(error) { // repeated error-handling logic
    console.log("Error: " + error);
});
```

Notice how in this example, each step of the process uses the same error-handling logic, but we've repeated the same code in several places. As always in programming, we should strive to avoid duplicating code. It's easy enough to abstract this out by defining an error-handling function in a shared scope:

```
function onError(error) {
    console.log("Error: " + error);
}

downloadAsync("a.txt", function(a) {
    downloadAsync("b.txt", function(b) {
        downloadAsync("c.txt", function(c) {
            console.log("Contents: " + a + b + c);
        }, onError);
    }, onError);
}, onError);
```

Of course, if we combine multiple steps into a single compound operation with utilities such as downloadAllAsync (as Items 62 and 66 recommend), we naturally end up only needing to provide a single error
callback:

```
downloadAllAsync(["a.txt", "b.txt", "c.txt"], function(abc) {
    console.log("Contents: " + abc[0] + abc[1] + abc[2]);
}, function(error) {
    console.log("Error: " + error);
});
```

Another style of error-handling API, popularized by the Node.js platform, takes only a single callback whose first argument is either an
error, if one occurred, or a falsy value such as null otherwise. For
these kinds of APIs, we can still define a common error-handling
function, but we need to guard each callback with an if statement:

```
function onError(error) {
    console.log("Error: " + error);
}

downloadAsync("a.txt", function(error, a) {
    if (error) {
        onError(error);
        return;
    }
    downloadAsync("b.txt", function(error, b) {
        // duplicated error-checking logic
        if (error) {
            onError(error);
            return;
        }
        downloadAsync(url3, function(error, c) {
            // duplicated error-checking logic
            if (error) {
                onError(error);
                return;
            }
            console.log("Contents: " + a + b + c);
        });
    });
});
```

In frameworks with this style of error callback, programmers often
abandon conventions requiring if statements to span multiple lines
with braced bodies, leading to more concise, less distracting error
handling:

```javascript
function onError(error) {
    console.log("Error: " + error);
}

downloadAsync("a.txt", function(error, a) {
    if (error) return onError(error);

    downloadAsync("b.txt", function(error, b) {
        if (error) return onError(error);

        downloadAsync(url3, function(error, c) {
            if (error) return onError(error);

            console.log("Contents: " + a + b + c);
        });
    });
});
```

Or, as always, combining steps with an abstraction helps eliminate duplication:

```javascript
var filenames = ["a.txt", "b.txt", "c.txt"];

downloadAllAsync(filenames, function(error, abc) {
    if (error) {
        console.log("Error: " + error);
        return;
    }
    console.log("Contents: " + abc[0] + abc[1] + abc[2]);
});
```

One of the practical differences between try...catch and typical error-handling logic in asynchronous APIs is that try makes it easier to define "catchall" logic so that it's difficult to forget to handle errors in an entire region of code. With asynchronous APIs like the one above, it's very easy to forget to provide error handling in any of the steps of the process. Often, this results in an error getting silently dropped. A program that ignores errors can be very frustrating for users: The application provides no feedback that something went wrong (sometimes resulting in a hanging progress notification that never clears). Similarly, silent errors are a nightmare to debug, since they provide no clues about the source of the problem. The best cure is prevention: Working with asynchronous APIs requires vigilance to make sure you handle all error conditions explicitly.

Things to Remember

✦ Avoid copying and pasting error-handling code by writing shared error-handling functions.

✦ Make sure to handle all error conditions explicitly to avoid dropped errors.

Item 64: Use Recursion for Asynchronous Loops

Consider a function that takes an array of URLs and tries to download one at a time until one succeeds. If the API were synchronous, it would be easy to implement with a loop:

```
function downloadOneSync(urls) {
    for (var i = 0, n = urls.length; i < n; i++) {
        try {
            return downloadSync(urls[i]);
        } catch (e) { }
    }
    throw new Error("all downloads failed");
}
```

But this approach won't work for downloadOneAsync, because we can't suspend a loop and resume it in a callback. If we tried using a loop, it would initiate all of the downloads rather than waiting for one to continue before trying the next:

```
function downloadOneAsync(urls, onsuccess, onerror) {
    for (var i = 0, n = urls.length; i < n; i++) {
        downloadAsync(urls[i], onsuccess, function(error) {
            // ?
        });
        // loop continues
    }
    throw new Error("all downloads failed");
}
```

So we need to implement something that acts like a loop, but that doesn't continue executing until we explicitly say so. The solution is to implement the loop as a function, so we can decide when to start each iteration:

```
function downloadOneAsync(urls, onsuccess, onfailure) {
    var n = urls.length;

    function tryNextURL(i) {
        if (i >= n) {
```

```
        onfailure("all downloads failed");
        return;
    }
    downloadAsync(urls[i], onsuccess, function() {
        tryNextURL(i + 1);
    });
    }

    tryNextURL(0);
}
```

The local `tryNextURL` function is *recursive:* Its implementation involves a call to itself. Now, in typical JavaScript environments, a recursive function that calls itself synchronously can fail after too many calls to itself. For example, this simple recursive function tries to call itself 100,000 times, but in most JavaScript environments it fails with a runtime error:

```
function countdown(n) {
    if (n === 0) {
        return "done";
    } else {
        return countdown(n - 1);
    }
}
```

```
countdown(100000); // error: maximum call stack size exceeded
```

So how could the recursive `downloadOneAsync` be safe if `countdown` explodes when n is too large? To answer this, let's take a small detour and unpack the error message provided by `countdown`.

JavaScript environments usually reserve a fixed amount of space in memory, known as the *call stack,* to keep track of what to do next after returning from function calls. Imagine executing this little program:

```
function negative(x) {
    return abs(x) * -1;
}
```

```
function abs(x) {
    return Math.abs(x);
}
```

```
console.log(negative(42));
```

At the point in the application where Math.abs is called with the argument 42, there are several other function calls in progress, each waiting for another to return. Figure 7.2 illustrates the call stack at this point. At the point of each function call, the bullet symbol (•) depicts the place in the program where a function call has occurred and where that call will return to when it finishes. Like the traditional stack data structure, this information follows a "last-in, first-out" protocol: The most recent function call that pushes information onto the stack (represented as the bottommost frame of the stack) will be the first to pop back off the stack. When Math.abs finishes, it returns to the abs function, which returns to the negative function, which in turn returns to the outermost script.

When a program is in the middle of too many function calls, it can run out of stack space, resulting in a thrown exception. This condition is known as *stack overflow*. In our example, calling countdown(100000) requires countdown to call itself 100,000 times, each time pushing another stack frame, as shown in Figure 7.3. The amount of space required to store so many stack frames exhausts the space allocated by most JavaScript environments, leading to a runtime error.

Now take another look at downloadOneAsync. Unlike countdown, which can't return until the recursive call returns, downloadOneAsync only calls itself from within an asynchronous callback. Remember that asynchronous APIs return immediately—before their callbacks are invoked. So downloadOneAsync returns, causing its stack frame to be popped off of the call stack, *before* any recursive call causes a new stack frame to be pushed back on the stack. (In fact, the callback is always invoked in a separate turn of the event loop, and each turn of the event loop invokes its event handler with the call stack initially

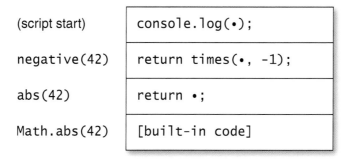

Figure 7.2 A call stack during the execution of a simple program

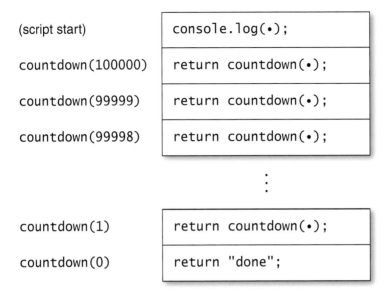

(script start)	`console.log(•);`
countdown(100000)	`return countdown(•);`
countdown(99999)	`return countdown(•);`
countdown(99998)	`return countdown(•);`

⋮

| countdown(1) | `return countdown(•);` |
| countdown(0) | `return "done";` |

Figure 7.3 A call stack during the execution of a recursive function

empty.) So downloadOneAsync never starts eating up call stack space, no matter how many iterations it requires.

Things to Remember

✦ Loops cannot be asynchronous.

✦ Use recursive functions to perform iterations in separate turns of the event loop.

✦ Recursion performed in separate turns of the event loop does not overflow the call stack.

Item 65: Don't Block the Event Queue on Computation

Item 61 explains how asynchronous APIs help to prevent a program from clogging up an application's event queue. But this is not the whole story. After all, as every programmer can tell you, it's easy enough to stall an application without even a single function call:

```
while (true) { }
```

And it doesn't take an infinite loop to write a sluggish program. Code takes time to run, and inefficient algorithms or data structures can lead to long-running computations.

Of course, efficiency is not a concern that's unique to JavaScript. But event-based programming does impose particular constraints. In order to preserve a high degree of interactivity in a client application, or to ensure that all incoming requests get adequately serviced in a server application, it's critical to keep each turn of the event loop as short as possible. Otherwise, the event queue can start getting backed up, growing at a faster rate than event handlers can be dispatched to shrink it again. In the browser setting, expensive computations also lead to a bad user experience, since a page's user interface is mostly unresponsive while JavaScript code is running.

So what can you do if your application needs to perform expensive computations? There's no one right answer, but there are a few common techniques available. Perhaps the simplest approach is to use a concurrency mechanism like the web client platform's Worker API. This can be a good approach for games with artificial intelligence that may need to search through a large space of possible moves. The game might start up by spawning a dedicated worker for computing moves:

```
var ai = new Worker("ai.js");
```

This has the effect of spawning a new concurrent thread of execution with its own separate event queue, using the source file ai.js as the worker's script. The worker runs in a completely isolated state: It has no direct access to any of the objects of the application. However, the application and worker can communicate with each other by sending *messages* to each other, in the form of strings. So whenever the game requires the computer to make a move, it can send a message to the worker:

```
var userMove = /* ... */;

ai.postMessage(JSON.stringify({
    userMove: userMove
}));
```

The argument to postMessage is added to the worker's event queue as a message. To process responses from the worker, the game registers an event handler:

```
ai.onmessage = function(event) {
    executeMove(JSON.parse(event.data).computerMove);
};
```

Meanwhile, the source file ai.js instructs the worker to listen for messages and perform the work required to compute next moves:

```
self.onmessage = function(event) {
    // parse the user move
    var userMove = JSON.parse(event.data).userMove;

    // generate the next computer move
    var computerMove = computeNextMove(userMove);

    // format the computer move
    var message = JSON.stringify({
        computerMove: computerMove
    });

    self.postMessage(message);
};

function computeNextMove(userMove) {
    // ...
}
```

Not all JavaScript platforms provide an API like Worker. And sometimes the overhead of passing messages can become too costly. A different approach is to break up an algorithm into multiple steps, each consisting of a manageable chunk of work. Consider the work-list algorithm from Item 48 for searching a social network graph:

```
Member.prototype.inNetwork = function(other) {
    var visited = {};
    var worklist = [this];
    while (worklist.length > 0) {
        var member = worklist.pop();
        // ...
        if (member === other) { // found?
            return true;
        }
        // ...
    }
    return false;
};
```

If the while loop at the heart of this procedure is too expensive, the search might block the application event queue for unacceptably long periods of time. Even if the Worker API is available, it might be expensive or inconvenient to implement, since it requires either copying the entire state of the network graph or storing the graph state in a worker and always using message passing to update and query the network.

Luckily, the algorithm is defined as a sequence of individual steps: the iterations of the while loop. We can convert inNetwork to an asynchronous function by adding a callback parameter and, as described in Item 64, replacing the while loop with an asynchronous, recursive function:

```
Member.prototype.inNetwork = function(other, callback) {
    var visited = {};
    var worklist = [this];
    function next() {
        if (worklist.length === 0) {
            callback(false);
            return;
        }
        var member = worklist.pop();
        // ...
        if (member === other) { // found?
            callback(true);
            return;
        }
        // ...
        setTimeout(next, 0); // schedule the next iteration
    }
    setTimeout(next, 0); // schedule the first iteration
};
```

Let's examine in detail how this code works. In place of the while loop, we've written a local function called next, which has the responsibility of performing a single iteration of the loop and then scheduling the next iteration to run asynchronously in the application event queue. This allows other events that have occurred in the meantime to be processed before continuing with the next iteration. When the search is complete, by either finding a match or exhausting the work-list, we call the callback with the result value and effectively complete the loop by returning from next without scheduling anymore iterations.

To schedule iterations, we are using the common setTimeout API, available in multiple JavaScript platforms, for registering next to run after a minimal amount of elapsed time (0 milliseconds). This has the effect of adding the callback to the event queue almost right away. It's worth noting that while setTimeout is relatively portable across platforms, there's often a better alternative available. In the browser setting, for example, it's actually throttled to a minimum timeout of 4 milliseconds, and there are alternatives using postMessage that enqueue an event immediately.

If performing only one iteration of the algorithm in each turn of the application event queue is overkill, we can tune the algorithm to perform a customized number of iterations per turn. This is easily accomplished with a simple counter loop surrounding the main portion of next:

```
Member.prototype.inNetwork = function(other, callback) {
    // ...
    function next() {
        for (var i = 0; i < 10; i++) {
            // ...
        }
        setTimeout(next, 0);
    }
    setTimeout(next, 0);
};
```

Things to Remember

✦ Avoid expensive algorithms in the main event queue.

✦ On platforms that support it, the Worker API can be used for running long computations in a separate event queue.

✦ When the Worker API is not available or is too costly, consider breaking up computations across multiple turns of the event loop.

Item 66: Use a Counter to Perform Concurrent Operations

Item 63 suggested the utility function downloadAllAsync to take an array of URLs and download them all, returning the array of file contents, one string per URL. Besides cleaning up nested callbacks, downloadAllAsync's primary benefit is downloading files *concurrently:* Instead of waiting for each file to finish downloading, we can initiate all the downloads at once, in a single turn of the event loop.

Concurrent logic is subtle and easy to get wrong. Here is an implementation with a devious little flaw:

```
function downloadAllAsync(urls, onsuccess, onerror) {
    var result = [], length = urls.length;

    if (length === 0) {
        setTimeout(onsuccess.bind(null, result), 0);
        return;
    }
```

```
    urls.forEach(function(url) {
        downloadAsync(url, function(text) {
            if (result) {
                // race condition
                result.push(text);
                if (result.length === urls.length) {
                    onsuccess(result);
                }
            }
        }, function(error) {
            if (result) {
                result = null;
                onerror(error);
            }
        });
    });
}
```

This function has a serious bug, but first let's look at how it works. We start by ensuring that if the input array is empty, the callback is invoked with an empty result array—if we didn't, neither of the two callbacks would ever be invoked, since the forEach loop would be empty. (Item 67 explains why we call setTimeout to invoke the onsuccess callback instead of calling it directly.) Next, we iterate over the URL array, requesting an asynchronous download for each. For each successful download, we add the file contents to the result array; if all URLs have been successfully downloaded, we call the onsuccess callback with the completed result array. If any download fails, we invoke the onerror callback with the error value. In case of multiple failed downloads, we also set the result array to null to make sure that onerror is only called once, for the first error that occurs.

To see what goes wrong, consider a use such as this:

```
var filenames = [
    "huge.txt",   // huge file
    "tiny.txt",   // tiny file
    "medium.txt" // medium-sized file
];
downloadAllAsync(filenames, function(files) {
    console.log("Huge file: " + files[0].length);   // tiny
    console.log("Tiny file: " + files[1].length);   // medium
    console.log("Medium file: " + files[2].length); // huge
}, function(error) {
    console.log("Error: " + error);
});
```

Since the files are downloaded concurrently, the events can occur (and consequently be added to the application event queue) in arbitrary orders. If, for example, `tiny.txt` completes first, followed by `medium.txt` and then `huge.txt`, the callbacks installed in `downloadAllAsync` will be called in a different order than the order they were created in. But the implementation of `downloadAllAsync` pushes each intermediate result onto the end of the `result` array as soon as it arrives. So `downloadAllAsync` produces an array containing downloaded files stored in an unknown order. It's almost impossible to use an API like that correctly, because the caller has no way to figure out which result is which. The example above, which assumes the results are in the same order as the input array, will fail completely in this case.

Item 48 introduced the idea of nondeterminism: unspecified behavior that programs cannot rely on without behaving unpredictably. Concurrent events are the most important source of nondeterminism in JavaScript. Specifically, *the order in which events occur* is not guaranteed to be the same from one execution of an application to the next.

When an application depends on the particular order of events to function correctly, the application is said to suffer from a *data race:* Multiple concurrent actions can modify a shared data structure differently depending on the order in which they occur. (Intuitively, the concurrent operations are "racing" against one another to see who will finish first.) Data races are truly sadistic bugs: They may not even show up in a particular test run, since running the same program twice may result in different behavior each time. For example, the user of `downloadAllAsync` might try to reorder the files based on which was more likely to download first:

```
downloadAllAsync(filenames, function(files) {
    console.log("Huge file: " + files[2].length);
    console.log("Tiny file: " + files[0].length);
    console.log("Medium file: " + files[1].length);
}, function(error) {
    console.log("Error: " + error);
});
```

In this case, the results might arrive in the same order most of the time, but from time to time, due perhaps to changing server loads or network caches, the files might not arrive in the expected order. These tend to be the most challenging bugs to diagnose, because they're so difficult to reproduce. Of course, we could go back to downloading the files sequentially, but then we lose the performance benefits of concurrency.

The solution is to implement downloadAllAsync so that it always pro-duces predictable results regardless of the unpredictable order of events. Instead of pushing each result onto the end of the array, we store it at its original index:

```
function downloadAllAsync(urls, onsuccess, onerror) {
    var length = urls.length;
    var result = [];

    if (length === 0) {
        setTimeout(onsuccess.bind(null, result), 0);
        return;
    }

    urls.forEach(function(url, i) {
        downloadAsync(url, function(text) {
            if (result) {
                result[i] = text; // store at fixed index

                // race condition
                if (result.length === urls.length) {
                    onsuccess(result);
                }
            }
        }, function(error) {
            if (result) {
                result = null;
                onerror(error);
            }
        });
    });
}
```

This implementation takes advantage of the forEach callback's second argument, which provides the array index for the current iteration. Unfortunately, it's still not correct. Item 51 describes the contract of array updates: Setting an indexed property always ensures that the array's length property is greater than that index. Imagine a request such as:

```
downloadAllAsync(["huge.txt", "medium.txt", "tiny.txt"]);
```

If the file tiny.txt finishes loading before one of the other files, the result array will acquire a property at index 2, which causes result.length to be updated to 3. The user's success callback will then be prematurely called with an incomplete array of results.

The correct implementation uses a counter to track the number of pending operations:

```
function downloadAllAsync(urls, onsuccess, onerror) {
    var pending = urls.length;
    var result = [];

    if (pending === 0) {
        setTimeout(onsuccess.bind(null, result), 0);
        return;
    }

    urls.forEach(function(url, i) {
        downloadAsync(url, function(text) {
            if (result) {
                result[i] = text; // store at fixed index
                pending--;         // register the success
                if (pending === 0) {
                    onsuccess(result);
                }
            }
        }, function(error) {
            if (result) {
                result = null;
                onerror(error);
            }
        });
    });
}
```

Now no matter what order the events occur in, the pending counter accurately indicates when all events have completed, and the complete results are returned in the proper order.

Things to Remember

✦ Events in a JavaScript application occur nondeterministically, that is, in unpredictable order.

✦ Use a counter to avoid data races in concurrent operations.

Item 67: Never Call Asynchronous Callbacks Synchronously

Imagine a variation of downloadAsync that keeps a cache (implemented as a Dict—see Item 45) to avoid downloading the same file multiple times. In the cases where the file is already cached, it's tempting to invoke the callback immediately:

```
var cache = new Dict();

function downloadCachingAsync(url, onsuccess, onerror) {
    if (cache.has(url)) {
        onsuccess(cache.get(url)); // synchronous call
        return;
    }
    return downloadAsync(url, function(file) {
        cache.set(url, file);
        onsuccess(file);
    }, onerror);
}
```

As natural as it may seem to provide data immediately if it's available, this violates the expectations of an asynchronous API's clients in subtle ways. First of all, it changes the expected order of operations. Item 62 showed the following example, which for a well-behaved asynchronous API should always log messages in a predictable order:

```
downloadAsync("file.txt", function(file) {
    console.log("finished");
});
console.log("starting");
```

With the naïve implementation of downloadCachingAsync above, such client code could end up logging the events in either order, depending on whether the file has been cached:

```
downloadCachingAsync("file.txt", function(file) {
    console.log("finished"); // might happen first
});
console.log("starting");
```

The order of logging messages is one thing. More generally, the purpose of asynchronous APIs is to maintain the strict separation of turns of the event loop. As Item 61 explains, this simplifies concurrency by alleviating code in one turn of the event loop from having to worry about other code changing shared data structures concurrently. An asynchronous callback that gets called synchronously violates this separation, causing code intended for a separate turn of the event loop to execute before the current turn completes.

For example, an application might keep a queue of files remaining to download and display a message to the user:

```
downloadCachingAsync(remaining[0], function(file) {
    remaining.shift();
    // ...
});
```

```
status.display("Downloading " + remaining[0] + "...");
```

If the callback is invoked synchronously, the display message will show the wrong filename (or worse, "undefined" if the queue is empty).

Invoking an asynchronous callback can cause even subtler problems. Item 64 explains that asynchronous callbacks are intended to be invoked with an essentially empty call stack, so it's safe to implement asynchronous loops as recursive functions without any danger of accumulating unbounded call stack space. A synchronous call negates this guarantee, making it possible for an ostensibly asynchronous loop to exhaust the call stack space. Yet another issue is exceptions: With the above implementation of downloadCachingAsync, if the callback throws an exception, it will be thrown in the turn of the event loop that initiated the download, rather than in a separate turn as expected.

To ensure that the callback is always invoked asynchronously, we can use an existing asynchronous API. Just as we did in Items 65 and 66, we use the common library function setTimeout to add a callback to the event queue after a minimum timeout. There may be preferable alternatives to setTimeout for scheduling immediate events, depending on the platform.

```
var cache = new Dict();
```

```
function downloadCachingAsync(url, onsuccess, onerror) {
    if (cache.has(url)) {
        var cached = cache.get(url);
        setTimeout(onsuccess.bind(null, cached), 0);
        return;
    }
    return downloadAsync(url, function(file) {
        cache.set(url, file);
        onsuccess(file);
    }, onerror);
}
```

We use bind (see Item 25) to save the result as the first argument for the onsuccess callback.

Things to Remember

✦ Never call an asynchronous callback synchronously, even if the data is immediately available.

✦ Calling an asynchronous callback synchronously disrupts the expected sequence of operations and can lead to unexpected interleaving of code.

✦ Calling an asynchronous callback synchronously can lead to stack overflows or mishandled exceptions.

✦ Use an asynchronous API such as setTimeout to schedule an asynchronous callback to run in another turn.

Item 68: Use Promises for Cleaner Asynchronous Logic

A popular alternative way to structure asynchronous APIs is to use *promises* (sometimes known as *deferreds* or *futures*). The asynchronous APIs we've discussed in this chapter take callbacks as arguments:

```
downloadAsync("file.txt", function(file) {
    console.log("file: " + file);
});
```

By contrast, a promise-based API does not take callbacks as arguments; instead, it returns a promise object, which itself accepts callbacks via its then method:

```
var p = downloadP("file.txt");

p.then(function(file) {
    console.log("file: " + file);
});
```

So far this hardly looks any different from the original version. But the power of promises is in their *composability*. The callback passed to then can be used not only to cause effects (in the above example, to print out to the console), but also to produce results. By returning a value from the callback, we can construct a new promise:

```
var fileP = downloadP("file.txt");

var lengthP = fileP.then(function(file) {
    return file.length;
});
```

```
lengthP.then(function(length) {
    console.log("length: " + length);
});
```

One way to think about a promise is as an object that represents an *eventual value*—it wraps a concurrent operation that may not have completed yet, but will eventually produce a result value. The then method allows us to take one promise object that represents one type of eventual value and generate a new promise object that represents another type of eventual value—whatever we return from the callback.

This ability to construct new promises from existing promises gives them great flexibility, and enables some simple but very powerful idioms. For example, it's relatively easy to construct a utility for "joining" the results of multiple promises:

```
var filesP = join(downloadP("file1.txt"),
                  downloadP("file2.txt"),
                  downloadP("file3.txt"));

filesP.then(function(files) {
    console.log("file1: " + files[0]);
    console.log("file2: " + files[1]);
    console.log("file3: " + files[2]);
});
```

Promise libraries also often provide a utility function called when, which can be used similarly:

```
var fileP1 = downloadP("file1.txt"),
    fileP2 = downloadP("file2.txt"),
    fileP3 = downloadP("file3.txt");

when([fileP1, fileP2, fileP3], function(files) {
    console.log("file1: " + files[0]);
    console.log("file2: " + files[1]);
    console.log("file3: " + files[2]);
});
```

Part of what makes promises an excellent level of abstraction is that they communicate their results by returning values from their then methods, or by composing promises via utilities such as join, rather than by writing to shared data structures via concurrent callbacks. This is inherently safer because it avoids the data races discussed in Item 66. Even the most conscientious programmer can make simple mistakes when saving the results of asynchronous operations in shared variables or data structures:

```
var file1, file2;

downloadAsync("file1.txt", function(file) {
    file1 = file;
});

downloadAsync("file2.txt", function(file) {
    file1 = file; // wrong variable
});
```

Promises avoid this kind of bug because the style of concisely composing promises avoids modifying shared data.

Notice also that sequential chains of asynchronous logic actually appear sequential with promises, rather than with the unwieldy nesting patterns demonstrated in Item 62. What's more, error handling is automatically propagated through promises. When you chain a collection of asynchronous operations together through promises, you can provide a single error callback for the entire sequence, rather than passing an error callback to every step as in the code in Item 63.

Despite this, it is sometimes useful to create certain kinds of races purposefully, and promises provide an elegant mechanism for doing this. For example, an application may need to try downloading the same file simultaneously from several different servers and take whichever one completes first. The select (or choose) utility takes several promises and produces a promise whose value is whichever result becomes available first. In other words, it "races" several promises against one another.

```
var fileP = select(downloadP("http://example1.com/file.txt"),
                   downloadP("http://example2.com/file.txt"),
                   downloadP("http://example3.com/file.txt"));

fileP.then(function(file) {
    console.log("file: " + file);
});
```

Another use of select is to provide timeouts to abort operations that take too long:

```
var fileP = select(downloadP("file.txt"), timeoutErrorP(2000));

fileP.then(function(file) {
    console.log("file: " + file);
}, function(error) {
    console.log("I/O error or timeout: " + error);
});
```

In that last example, we're demonstrating the mechanism for providing error callbacks to a promise as the second argument to then.

Things to Remember

+ Promises represent eventual values, that is, concurrent computations that eventually produce a result.

+ Use promises to compose different concurrent operations.

+ Use promise APIs to avoid data races.

+ Use select (also known as choose) for situations where an intentional race condition is required.

Index